W9-CAG-250

SINGER

SEWING REFERENCE LIBRARY®

Creating Fashion Accessories

Cy DeCosse Incorporated
Minnetonka, Minnesota

SINGER

SEWING REFERENCE LIBRARY®

Creating Fashion Accessories

Contents

Copyright © 1993
Cy DeCosse Incorporated
5900 Green Oak Drive
Minnetonka, Minnesota 55343
1-800-328-3895
All rights reserved
Printed in Mexico

CREATING FASHION ACCESSORIES
Created by: The Editors of Cy DeCosse
Incorporated, in cooperation with
the Sewing Education Department,
Singer Sewing Company. Singer is a
trademark of The Singer Company and
is used under license.

Library of Congress
Cataloging-in-Publication Data

Creating fashion accessories.

p. cm. — (Singer sewing reference
library)
Includes index.
ISBN 0-86573-284-1
ISBN 0-86573-285-X (pbk.)
1. Dress accessories.   I. Series.
TT560.C74 1993
646.4'8 — dc20   92-32804

CY DECOSSE INCORPORATED
Chairman: Cy DeCosse
President: James B. Maus
Executive Vice President: William B. Jones

Also available from the publisher:
*Sewing Essentials, Sewing for the Home,
Clothing Care & Repair, Sewing for Style,
Sewing Specialty Fabrics, Sewing
Activewear, The Perfect Fit, Timesaving
Sewing, More Sewing for the Home,
Tailoring, Sewing for Children, Sewing
with an Overlock, 101 Sewing Secrets,
Sewing Pants That Fit, Quilting by
Machine, Decorative Machine Stitching,
Creative Sewing Ideas, Sewing Lingerie,
Sewing Projects for the Home, Sewing
with Knits, More Creative Sewing Ideas,
Quilt Projects by Machine, Quick & Easy
Sewing Projects, Sewing for Special
Occasions, Sewing for the Holidays*

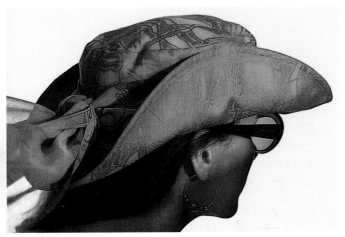

Executive Editor: Zoe A. Graul
Technical Director: Rita C. Opseth
Project Manager: Joseph Cella
Senior Art Director: Delores J. Swanson
Art Director: Linda Schloegel
Writer: Lori Ritter
Editor: Janice Cauley
Sample Coordinator: Carol Olson
Styling Director: Bobbette Destiche
Technical Photo Director: Bridget Haugh
Fabric Editor: Joanne Wawra
Assistant Fabric Editors: Holly Clements,
    Karin Enisman, Shelly Holl, Ann
    Stuart
Sewing Staff: Phyllis Galbraith, Bridget
    Haugh, Sara Macdonald, Linda
    Neubauer, Carol Olson, Carol Pilot,
    Nancy Sundeen, Barb Vik
Director of Development Planning
    & Production: Jim Bindas

Production Manager: Amelia Merz
Studio Manager: Cathleen Shannon
Assistant Studio Manager: Rena Tassone
Lead Photographer: Rex Irmen
Photographers: Rebecca Hawthorne,
    John Lauenstein, Mark Macemon,
    Paul Najlis, Mike Parker
Contributing Photographers: Phil Aarestad,
    Alan Mathiowetz, Chuck Nields, Brad
    Parker
Photo Stylist: Susan Pasqual
Electronic Publishing Specialist: Joe Fahey
Production Staff: Stephanie Beck, Diane
    Dreon-Krattiger, Adam Esco, Melissa
    Grabanski, Eva Hanson, Jim Huntley,
    Phil Juntti, Paul Najlis, Robert
    Powers, Mike Schauer, Greg Wallace,
    Nik Wogstad
Consultants: Ann Fatigati, Wendy Fedie,
    Pamela Hastings, Lynn Hazelton,

Barbara Hjort, Marcia Kelly, Kristi
Kuhnau, Gayle Liman, Lydia Lopez,
Linda Nakashima, Linda Neubauer,
Lindsey Peterson, Suzanne Stout,
Barbara Sykes, Melanie Teig-Schwolert,
Kathy Tilton, Barbara Vik
Contributors: C. M. Offray & Son, Inc.;
    Coats & Clark Inc.; Dyno
    Merchandise Corporation; EZ
    International; Fairfield Processing
    Corporation; HTC-Handler Textile
    Corporation; Olfa® Products
    International; Spartex Inc.; Streamline
    Industries, Inc.; Swiss-Metrosene, Inc.
Printed on American paper by: R. R.
Donnelley & Sons Co. (0195)

Introduction

Fashion accessories are the finishing touch for any outfit. Worn with a basic dress, they add the detailing that makes a special ensemble. They can dress up a suit or add whimsy to casual sportswear.

Making your own fashion accessories allows you to express your personal style, coordinating the colors and details so they work well with your garments. *Creating Fashion Accessories* offers inspiration as well as step-by-step instructions for belts, purses, scarves, hats, hair accessories, and more.

In the Belts and Bags section, we start by introducing a range of belt styles. Make a classic synthetic suede belt, personalized with an inset panel of quilting or punchneedle embroidery. Embellish a comfortable elasticized belt with hand-sewn beading, or trim one with fine decorative cordings that are couched in place with machine stitching. Twist your choice of yarns into rope belts, adding creative buckles, like seashells or clustered antique buttons.

Next, handbags are featured in several sizes and shapes. For an evening bag, sew a drawstring pouch in an elegant fabric with luxurious trims. Or if you need a classic handbag, sew a clutch with a zippered divider. You may prefer a basic clutch bag, or one that is personalized with custom embellishments. For casual activities, from shopping to swimming to health club workouts, carry a generous-sized tote bag with pockets. Confetti bags, randomly splashed with colorful trims, can be made in any size, from small coin purses to totes.

In the Scarves and Ties section, you will learn the basics for making your own square and rectangular scarves, including the recommended edge finishes appropriate for each fabric type and how to add decorative touches. For unique scarves that express your own creativity, follow the special instructions for hand-dyeing silk fabric using the salt technique. Then learn new, easy ways to wear scarves at the neck, waist, and hips — even ways to wear scarves as shawls. Also included in this section are the simple steps for making creative reversible ties that resemble men's ties, adding femininity and flair.

The Hats and Hair Accessories section includes a simple-to-sew hat that can be embellished and worn in a variety of ways. In addition to hats, this section covers hair accessories, from ponytail wraps to hair bows. Fabric-covered barrettes and headbands, as varied as the selection of fabrics available, are versatile for everyday wear. For special occasions, try the beaded barrettes or the delicate chiffon hair bows.

The final section, Jewelry and More, will inspire you as it teaches you jewelry-making techniques. Learn to create earrings, necklaces, bracelets, and even buttons from polymer clay, a modeling compound that can be oven-baked. Or make jewelry from bits of fabrics and fibers, including origami-style earrings and pins, collage jewelry, leather jewelry, and fabric-wrapped bracelets. There are also wire mesh earrings, woven with narrow strips of leather or fabrics. And to complete an outfit, discover ways to embellish sunglasses, gloves, and shoes to create unique designer accessories.

Belts & Bags

Suede Belts

A belt with a creative insert is a one-of-a-kind accessory. The belt is made from mediumweight synthetic suede, such as Ultrasuede®, and has a decorative insert. For a tailored look, use a simple pieced or quilted insert. For a more contemporary style, embellish the insert with punchneedle embroidery (page 37) or with a fabric collage (page 113).

The belt has a finished width of 1½" (3.8 cm), making it comfortable to wear. Hook and loop tape fastens the belt and allows for fitting adjustments.

When laying out synthetic suede, determine the desired nap direction. Secure the layers by pushing fine pins vertically through the pattern and fabric into the cutting board. Or use pattern weights to hold the pattern in place. For easy assembly, the belt facing is cut slightly wider than the belt front; the edges are trimmed evenly after they are stitched together.

YOU WILL NEED

6" (15 cm) mediumweight synthetic suede, 45" (115 cm) wide, for waists up to 31" (78.5 cm), or 10" (25.5 cm) synthetic suede, for waists larger than 31" (78.5 cm).

Hair canvas interfacing, yardage equal to waist measurement plus 6" (15 cm).

Paper-backed fusible web, yardage equal to waist measurement plus 6" (15 cm).

4" × 8" (10 × 20.5 cm) piece of lining fabric to match suede.

6" (15 cm) length of hook and loop tape, 1" (2.5 cm) wide, for closure.

3½" (9 cm) length of grosgrain ribbon, ¼" (6 mm) wide, for belt carrier.

4" × 8" (10 × 20.5 cm) piece of polyester fleece, for insert padding.

Suede belts may be embellished with jewelry, such as the button pin (page 105) on the belt at left, or the leather pin (page 114) on the belt at right.

Patterns for the Shaped Ends of a Suede Belt

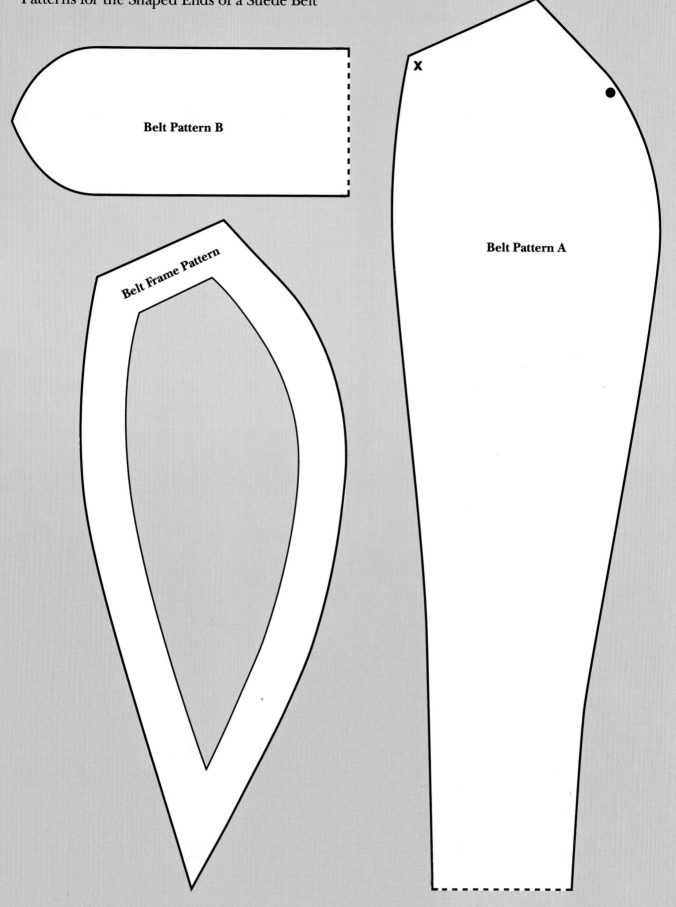

Belt Pattern B

Belt Pattern A

X

Belt Frame Pattern

How to Complete the Pattern for a Suede Belt

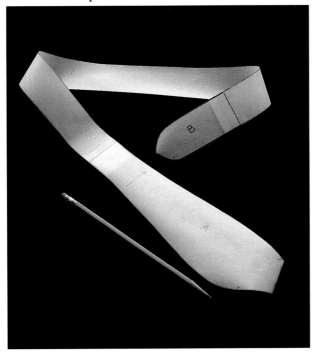

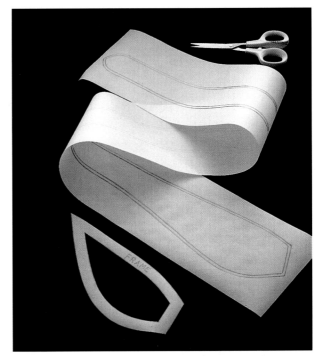

1) Trace pattern pieces A and B, opposite, onto tracing paper. On another piece of tracing paper, draw parallel lines 1½" (3.8 cm) apart; align pieces A and B on lines so the completed pattern length is equal to waist measurement plus 6" (15 cm).

2) Make pattern for interfacing and fusible web by tracing completed belt pattern from step 1 onto tracing paper and cutting it ⅛" (3 mm) smaller on all edges. Trace belt frame pattern, opposite.

How to Sew a Suede Belt

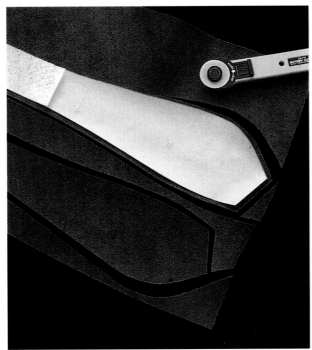

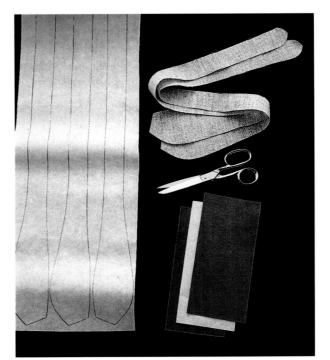

1) Cut one belt front from suede, using completed pattern from step 1, above; mark X on wrong side of suede and mark dot on right side. With pattern face down, cut one belt facing from suede, cutting it ⅛" (3 mm) larger on all edges.

2) Cut two pieces of interfacing and three pieces of paper-backed fusible web, using pattern from step 2, above; place pattern face down when cutting one of the pieces of fusible web. Cut 4" × 8" (10 × 20.5 cm) piece from suede, lining, and fusible web, for frame.

(Continued on next page)

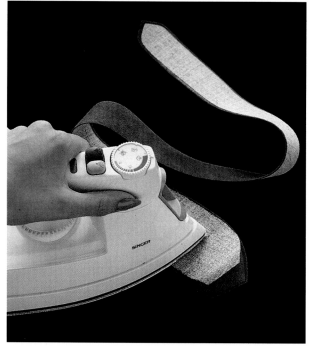

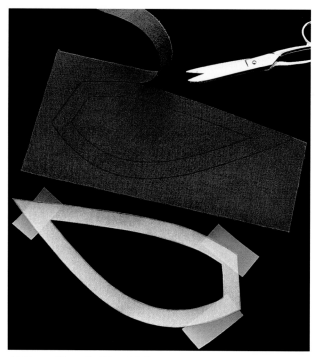

3) Fuse one piece of interfacing to wrong side of belt front, using fusible web according to manufacturer's directions and centering layers on belt. Repeat for belt facing.

4) Fuse 4" × 8" (10 × 20.5 cm) pieces of lining and suede together, using fusible web. With pattern for frame face down on lining side of fused piece, mark cutting lines, using pencil. Cut one frame, following marked lines.

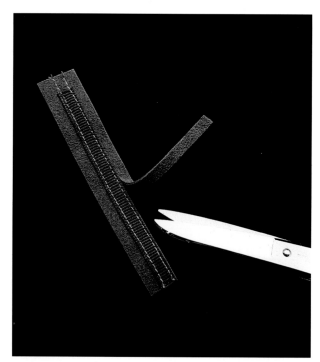

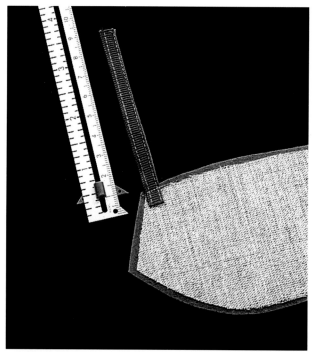

5) Edgestitch 3½" (9 cm) length of grosgrain ribbon to a scrap of suede, for belt carrier. Trim suede close to ribbon.

6) Position the belt carrier, suede side down, at marked X on wrong side of belt front, with the edges overlapping ⅜" (1 cm); stitch in place ⅛" (3 mm) from edge of belt.

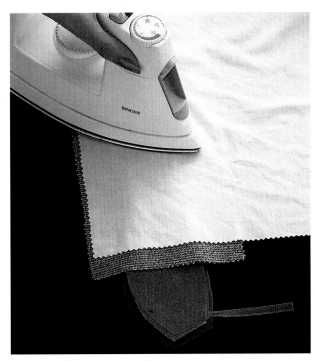

7) Glue-baste loop side of hook and loop tape on right side of belt facing, centering it 1¼" (3.2 cm) from wide end; edgestitch around tape.

8) Fuse belt front to belt facing, wrong sides together, using fusible web, making sure interfacing edges are concealed. Cover with piece of wool or flannel fabric, then with dampened press cloth; fuse for 20 seconds. Allow belt to cool before moving it.

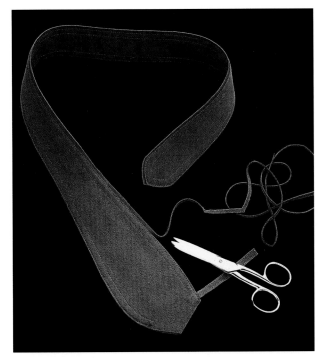

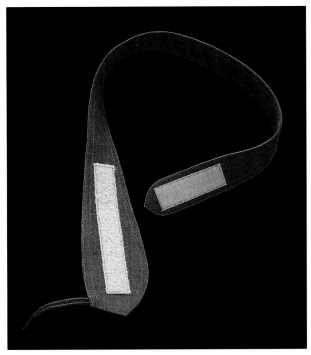

9) Edgestitch around belt, leaving end of belt open between dot and belt carrier. Stitch again ¼" (6 mm) from previous stitching. Trim belt facing even with belt front.

10) Trim hook side of hook and loop tape to 3" (7.5 cm); glue-baste to belt front, centering it ⅝" (1.5 cm) from narrow end. Edgestitch around tape.

(Continued on next page)

11) Fold belt carrier to facing side of belt, and align end with dot; trim carrier parallel to edge of belt, leaving ⅜" (1 cm) extending beyond edge.

12) Make desired insert, opposite. Using basting tape or glue stick, baste frame to insert; then baste framed insert to belt front.

13) Edgestitch around inner edge of frame, starting at tapered point; keep carrier free. If making belt with punchneedle insert, use zipper foot.

14) Edgestitch around outer edge of frame, starting at tapered point and stitching past carrier to opposite point; with needle down, fold carrier to facing side of belt. Insert end of carrier between frame and belt at dot; continue stitching around frame, stitching through carrier.

How to Sew a Pieced Insert

1) Cut fleece slightly larger than frame. Cut suede strips, and place on fleece, overlapping edges ¼" (6 mm); baste, using basting tape. Edgestitch strips to fleece.

2) Center the frame pattern over insert piece, and mark along outer edge, using pencil.

3) Stitch ¼" (6 mm) inside the marked line. Trim excess fabric close to stitching.

How to Sew a Quilted Insert

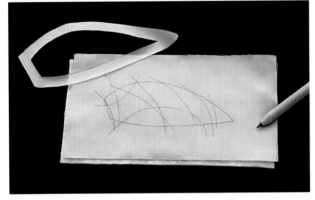 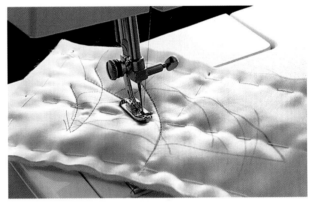

1) Cut fleece and fabric slightly larger than frame. Mark design area on fabric along inner edge of frame, using chalk. Mark quilting lines as desired, extending lines beyond design area.

2) Baste fabric to fleece; quilt on design lines. Finish insert, following steps 2 and 3, above. (Markings are exaggerated to show detail.)

How to Sew a Punchneedle Insert

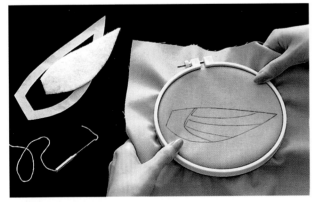 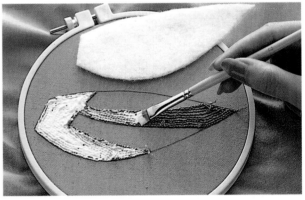

1) Mark design area for punchneedle on fleece and medium-weave fabric, following inner edge of frame. Cut fleece on marked line. Place fabric in embroidery hoop; check for distortion of design, and redraw outer design line, if necessary.

2) Make punchneedle design (page 37) as desired. Apply fabric glue to back of punchneedle design. Secure fleece to punchneedle, matching edges to design. Allow to dry. Remove from hoop; cut insert ¼" (6 mm) larger than fleece.

Elasticized Belts

A belt with an elasticized back and a shaped front panel is comfortable and versatile. The elastic is concealed in a shirred fabric casing. Make a belt to match a garment, or make one in a contrasting fabric. If desired, the panel can be embellished with couching or beading (page 23). Choose a lightweight to mediumweight fabric and a soft knitted elastic for an attractive, comfortable shirred casing. The front panel is stiffened with a fusible interfacing intended for crafts.

YOU WILL NEED

⅜ yd. (0.35 m) fabric for waists up to 30" (76 cm); or ½ yd. (0.5 m) fabric for waists 30" to 37" (76 to 94 cm).

¼ yd. (0.25 m) fusible interfacing intended for crafts.

25" (63.5 cm) length of knitted elastic, 1½" (3.8 cm) wide, for waists up to 30" (76 cm), or 29" (73.5 cm) for waists 30" to 37" (76 to 94 cm).

7" (18 cm) length of firm waistband interfacing, such as Armoflexxx®, 1½" (3.8 cm) wide.

2" (5 cm) length of hook and loop tape, 1" (2.5 cm) wide.

Narrow trims or cordings, for couched belt.

Beads and beading needle, for beaded belt.

Embellishments, such as couching (above) or beading (below), can be
added to the shaped front panel of an elasticized belt.

19

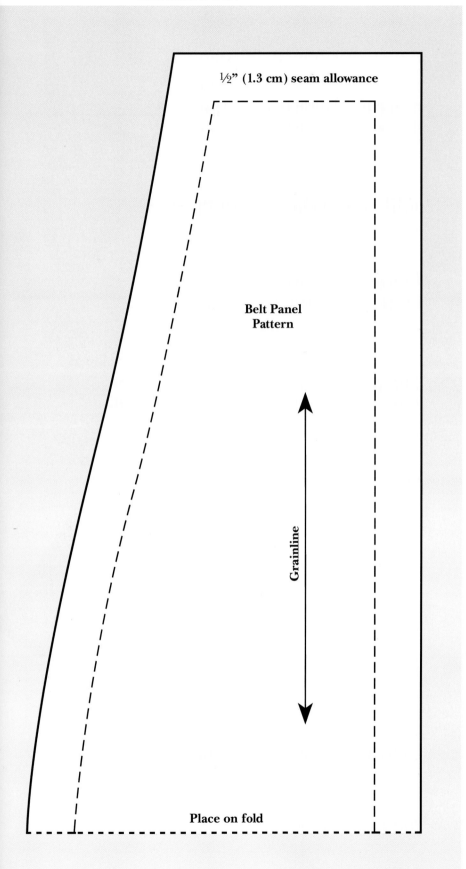

½" (1.3 cm) seam allowance

**Belt Panel
Pattern**

Grainline

Place on fold

1) Trace pattern, left, onto tracing paper, following solid lines; cut one belt panel and one panel facing.

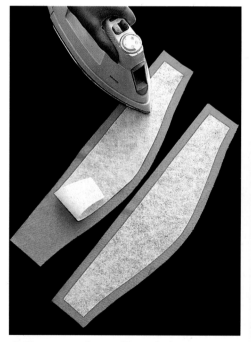

4) Fuse one piece of interfacing to the wrong side of the belt panel, centering it on panel. Repeat for panel facing. Embellish panel with couching (page 23), if desired.

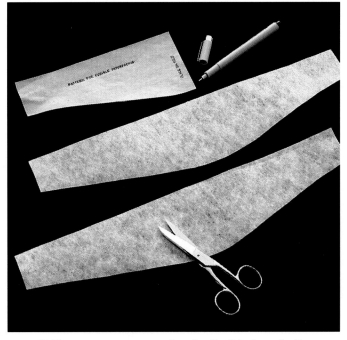

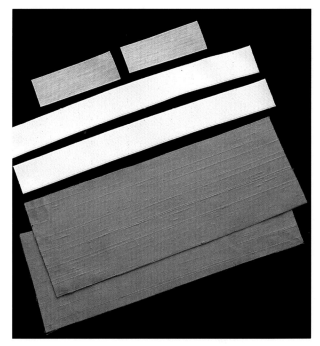

2) Trace pattern, opposite, for fusible interfacing, following dotted lines; cut two pieces of fusible interfacing.

3) Cut two rectangles for belt back, 4⅜" × 12" (11.2 × 30.5 cm) for waists up to 30" (76 cm), or 4⅜" × 14" (11.2 × 35.5 cm) for waists 30" to 37" (76 to 94 cm). Cut two pieces of elastic ½" (1.3 cm) longer than belt back pieces. Cut two 3½" (9 cm) strips of waistband interfacing, 1½" (3.8 cm) wide.

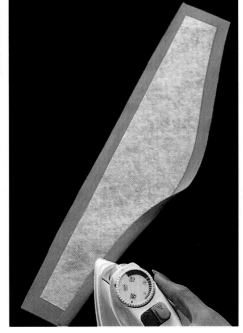

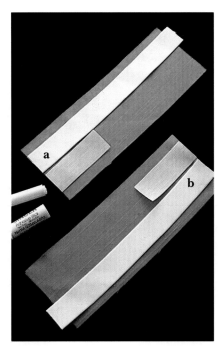

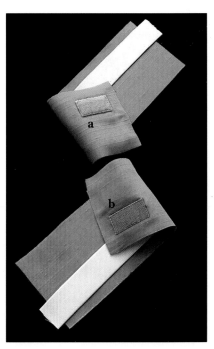

5) Press ½" (1.3 cm) seam allowance on lower curved edge of panel to wrong side. Repeat for panel facing.

6) Place elastic and interfacing on wrong side of right back **(a)** and left back **(b),** as shown, with long edges ⅝" (1.5 cm) from edges of fabric; glue-baste to seam allowance at end. These seam allowances will be at ends of belt.

7) Glue-baste loop side of hook and loop tape on right side of right back **(a),** 1" (2.5 cm) from end; edgestitch around tape, stitching through fabric and elastic. Repeat for hook side of hook and loop tape on left back **(b).**

(Continued on next page)

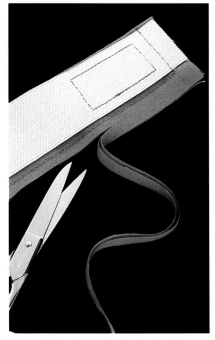

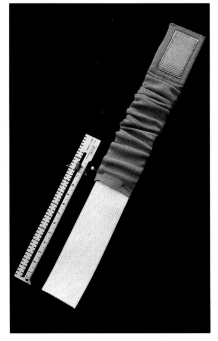

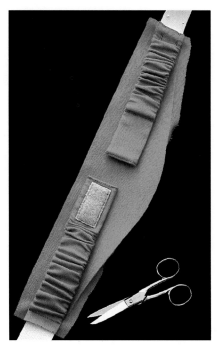

8) Fold one belt back in half lengthwise, right sides together. Stitch ½" (1.3 cm) seam along long edge and end. Trim corners and seam allowances. Repeat for remaining belt back.

9) Turn belt backs right side out. Topstitch edges at the ends of belt; topstitch again 2½" (6.5 cm) from ends. Pull elastic from belt backs, leaving 4½" (11.5 cm) extending beyond raw edge of casing; pin.

10) Pin belt backs to ends of panel, right sides together, as shown; seams are at upper edge of belt. Try on belt, and adjust elastic, if necessary. Stitch seams; trim excess elastic.

11) Pin panel facing to belt panel, right sides together, sandwiching belt backs between panels. Stitch ½" (1.3 cm) seams along ends and upper edge. Trim corners, and grade seam allowances.

12) Turn belt right side out; press. Embellish panel with beading, opposite, if desired. Slipstitch panel facing and belt panel together along curved edge. If desired, edgestitch around panel.

How to Sew a Couched Belt Panel

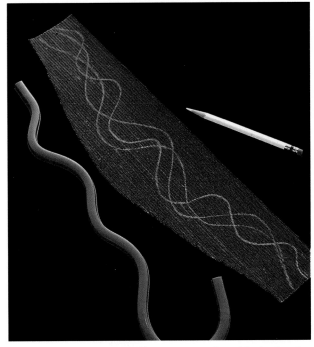

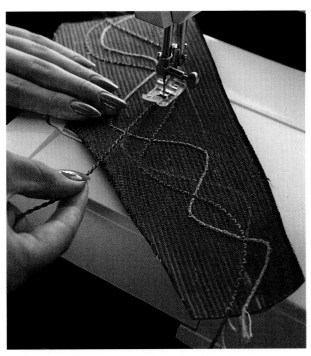

1) Mark random design lines on interfaced belt panel as desired, using flexible curve and chalk or water-soluble marking pen.

2) Zigzag over narrow trim or cording, following a design line and just catching fabric on both sides of trim; extend ends of trim and stitching into seam allowances.

How to Sew a Beaded Belt Panel

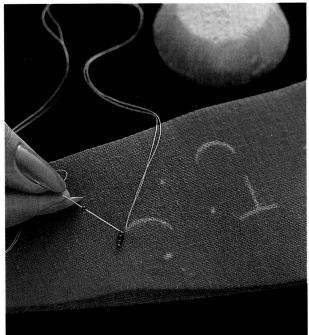

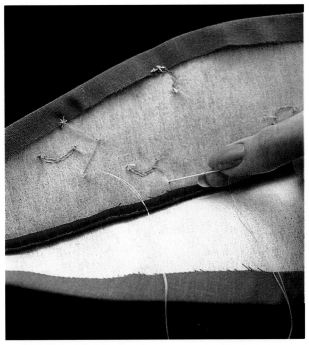

1) Apply a row of beads with backstitches, using a beading needle and double strand of waxed cotton-wrapped polyester thread. Bring needle up through bead on right side of fabric, then down through fabric. Take a stitch forward the width of one bead from first bead. Pull thread through bead; then take a stitch *backward* and down through fabric.

2) Stitch scattered beads by securing them with one or two stitches through bead; secure threads on wrong side by taking short stitch and pulling thread through loop. Carry thread between beads.

Rope Belts

Rope belts are comfortable to wear and simple to make. The wide selection of yarns that are available makes it easy to design a belt that matches or coordinates with a fabric. Use one type of yarn, or combine yarns for ropes of various colors and textures.

For a basic rope belt, simply knot and fringe the ends. Depending on the length, the belt may be either single-wrapped or double-wrapped around the waist. A single-wrapped basic belt should be long enough to wrap around the waist, plus extra for tying a knot or loose bow. A double-wrapped basic belt should be twice the waist measurement, plus extra for tying.

For an embellished rope belt, add a shell with drilled holes, or button jewelry (page 105); glue D-rings to the jewelry item or design it with holes for inserting the rope. These belts, made from two lengths of rope, are double-wrapped and tied in the front next to the embellishment. Each of the two lengths should be long enough to wrap around the waist, plus extra for tying.

Rope belts can be made quickly and easily by twisting strands of yarn by hand, as on pages 26 and 27. Decide how many strands you will need to achieve the desired diameter; the finished rope will be twice the diameter of the combined cut strands. The strands of yarn are cut two and one-half times the desired finished length of the rope. An easy-to-use specialized tool designed for making rope belts (below) is also available.

YOU WILL NEED

Yarn in one or more colors and textures.
Embellishment, if desired.

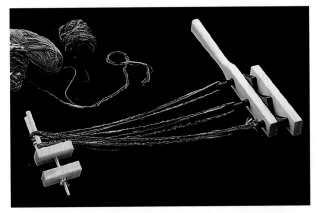

Roping tools are available at specialty yarn shops. Follow the manufacturer's directions, stringing the yarn through a set of hooks and pegs, then twisting a turn bar to form the rope.

Embellished rope belts are made from two lengths of rope attached to a shell, button jewelry item, or other embellishment. When worn, these double-wrapped belts wrap around the waist, crisscross in the back, and tie in front near the embellishment. Each of the two finished rope lengths should be long enough to wrap comfortably around the waist, plus extra for tying.

How to Make a Basic Rope Belt

1) Cut strands of yarn 2½ times the desired length of the finished rope; cut a sufficient number of strands to equal one-half the desired rope diameter. Knot end, and secure to padded, stationary surface, or have an assistant hold one end.

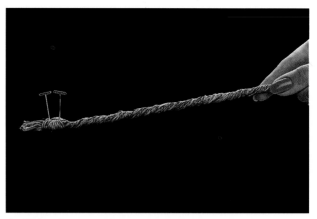

2) Twist the strands of yarn tightly, almost until the cord begins to crimp.

3) Pinch the cord at center point. Bring the two ends together, holding them taut to keep the cord from untwisting.

4) Pinch both sections about 10" (25.5 cm) from the looped end; allow sections to twist into a single rope. Continue pinching at 10" (25.5 cm) intervals, allowing sections to twist together. Knot ends. Smooth rope to even out twists.

5) Tie overhand knots the desired distance from the ends of the rope. Cut rope about 5" (12.5 cm) below knots; untwist rope. Twist each of two or three strands of yarn in clockwise direction.

6) Hold twisted strands of yarn together; twist in counterclockwise direction. Knot end, adding a bead, if desired. Repeat for remaining strands.

How to Make an Embellished Rope Belt

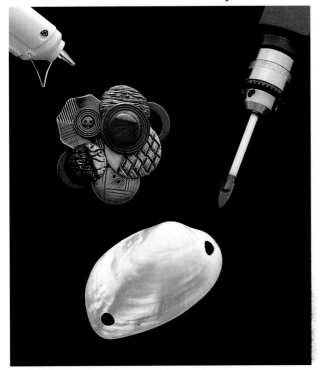

1) Make an embellishment as for button jewelry (page 105), designing it with holes for inserting the rope. Or use a seashell as an embellishment, drilling holes in the shell with a ceramic drill bit.

2) Cut strands of yarn 2½ times the desired length of finished rope; cut strands in half. Knot end, and secure to padded, stationary surface, or have an assistant hold one end.

3) Twist strands as in step 2, opposite. Feed twisted cord through embellishment to center of cord. Bring ends together and finish the rope as in steps 3 to 6, opposite. Repeat for remaining length of rope on other side of embellishment.

4) Wear belt by wrapping ropes around waist, with embellishment in center front and ropes crisscrossed in back. Knot belt in front near embellishment.

Drawstring Evening Bags

Create an elegant pouch for special occasions. Twisted cording and a decorative bead add a finishing touch to the bag. Make your own custom cording to match the fabric (page 25), or use purchased decorative cording.

Mediumweight fabrics that drape well, such as velvet and velveteen, work well. Other suitable fabrics include brocade, satin, and some tapestries. Lightweight fabrics may also be used; to add body and support, underline a lightweight fabric with batiste, or fuse a lightweight knit interfacing to the fabric.

YOU WILL NEED

⅜ yd. (0.35 m) **outer fabric.**

⅜ yd. (0.35 m) **lining fabric.**

2⅝ yd. (2.4 m) **decorative cording,** for trim and drawstrings.

1½ yd. (1.4 m) **decorative cording,** for shoulder strap.

Plastic canvas.

End caps.

Decorative bead and headpin, optional.

Contrasting casings and linings add interest to these elegant evening bags.

How to Sew a Drawstring Evening Bag

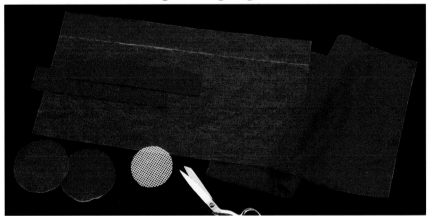

1) Cut one 11" × 21" (28 × 53.5 cm) rectangle from outer fabric; mark a line on the right side of the fabric 2¼" (6 cm) from upper long edge. Cut two 2" × 11" (5 × 28 cm) casing strips from lining fabric, as shown, or from outer fabric. Cut one 12½" × 21" (31.8 × 53.5 cm) rectangle from lining fabric. Cut one circle with 4¼" (10.8 cm) diameter from outer fabric and lining fabric. Cut one circle with 3¼" (8.2 cm) diameter from plastic canvas.

(Continued on next page)

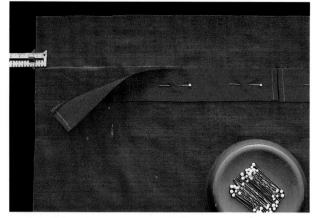

2) Stitch ¼" (6 mm) double-fold hem at short ends of casing strips; press under ¼" (6 mm) on long edges. Pin casing strips to rectangle from outer fabric, with upper fold on marked line and hemmed ends ½" (1.3 cm) from short sides; strips meet at center.

3) Stitch close to folded edges of casing strips; do not stitch ends. Topstitch decorative cording along upper and lower edges of casing; use open-toe foot or special-purpose foot with groove. Tape ends of cording to prevent raveling.

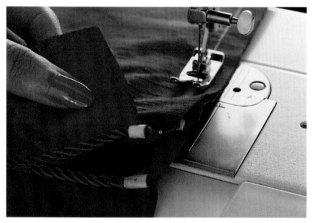

4) Fold rectangle, right sides together, matching the short ends; stitch ½" (1.3) seam, taking care not to catch casings in stitching.

5) Stitch two rows of gathering stitches ⅜" (1 cm) and ½" (1.3 cm) from lower edge; pin-mark edge into fourths. Pin-mark circle from outer fabric into fourths.

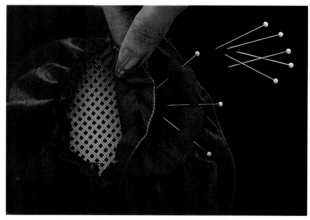

6) Pin circle to the lower edge, right sides together, matching pin marks; pull gathering threads, and adjust gathers to fit circle. Stitch ½" (1.3 cm) seam allowance; stitch again close to previous stitches.

7) Stitch ½" (1.3 cm) from edge of lining circle; press along stitched line. Place circle of plastic canvas on bottom of bag, inside seam allowance. Pin lining circle, wrong side down, over plastic canvas; slipstitch in place.

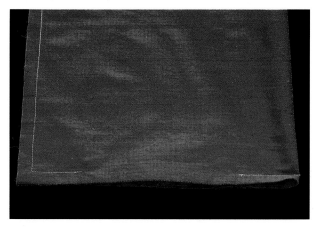

8) Cut cording for shoulder strap to desired length; tape ends before cutting, to prevent raveling. Position one end of strap on right side of purse at side seam, matching raw edges; stitch ⅜" (1 cm) from edge. Position other end of strap at opposite side; stitch.

9) Fold the lining fabric in half crosswise, right sides together; stitch ½" (1.3 cm) seam on side and bottom, leaving 6" (15 cm) opening on bottom, and leaving top completely open.

10) Pin lining to purse, with right sides together and raw edges even; to reduce bulk, place lining side seam opposite purse side seam. Stitch ½" (1.3 cm) seam.

11) Turn purse right side out through opening in lining; machine-stitch opening closed. Press upper edge of purse; edgestitch.

12) Cut cording for drawstring into two 26" (66 cm) cords. Using bodkin, feed one cord through casings, beginning and ending at one side. Repeat for remaining cord, beginning and ending at opposite side. Glue end caps to cords. Knot cords together.

13) Thread bead as desired on headpin; insert pin into the cording at center front of purse. Using needlenose pliers, form headpin into loop; wrap end of wire around loop to secure.

Clutch Purses

A classic clutch that coordinates with a garment completes an outfit. The flap can be shaped and embellished in a number of ways, making the design possibilities for this purse unlimited. Make a variety of pins to change the look of one basic clutch. Or for an elegant one-of-a-kind look, embellish the flap with punchneedle embroidery, creating a plush, raised design on woven fabric.

The lined purse is constructed with a zippered divider. A coat snap provides a simple closure. If desired, a shoulder strap can be attached.

Choose a mediumweight to heavyweight outer fabric; decorator fabrics have good body and are treated to repel soil. For added support, interface the outer and lining fabrics. Choose a crisp sew-in interfacing for the outer fabric and an all-purpose fusible interfacing for the lining.

To embellish the flap of a purse with punchneedle embroidery, mark the flap section on the fabric and embroider the design before cutting out the flap. The punchneedle is done using special needles, such as Igolochkoy™ needles, available in several sizes to accommodate a variety of fabrics and threads. The needles have an adjustable depth gauge, allowing you to change the depth of the pile.

YOU WILL NEED

½ yd. (0.5 m) outer fabric.

½ yd. (0.5 m) lining fabric.

⅔ yd. (0.63 m) each of sew-in and fusible interfacings.

9" (23 cm) zipper.

One coat snap.

Two D-rings, about ½" (1.3 cm) in diameter, two self-closing clasps, and chain, for optional shoulder strap.

Punchneedle and embroidery threads, for punchneedle embellishment.

Punchneedle embroidery can be stitched following a pattern for embroidery work (left). Or use punchneedle to emphasize the design in a patterned fabric (right).

33

How to Sew a Clutch Purse

1) **Cut** one 12" × 22" (30.5 × 56 cm) piece from outer fabric, lining, and interfacings, to be used for flap/back/divider. If flap will be embellished with punchneedle embroidery, mark, but do not cut, purse dimensions on outer fabric; this allows outer fabric to be placed in a hoop.

2) **Apply** fusible interfacing to wrong side of lining. Mark foldline of flap 15¼" (38.7 cm) from one short end of outer fabric and lining pieces; determine and mark shape of flap. Work punchneedle design, if desired (page 37). Baste sew-in interfacing to outer fabric. Cut flaps, allowing ¼" (6 mm) seam allowances.

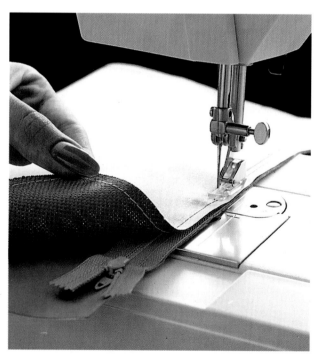

3) **Cut** one 12" × 15½" (30.5 × 39.3 cm) piece from outer fabric, lining, and interfacings, to be used for front/divider. Cut one 1¾" × 4" (4.5 × 10 cm) fabric strip for D-ring tabs. Apply fusible interfacing to the wrong side of lining piece; baste sew-in interfacing to wrong side of outer fabric.

4) **Center** zipper on one short end of lining piece for front/divider, right sides together, aligning raw edge of fabric to edge of zipper tape; glue-baste. Place outer fabric right side down over lining, sandwiching the zipper between the layers; glue-baste. Stitch ¼" (6 mm) seam.

5) Pin the lining and outer fabric together at opposite short end of front/divider, right sides together; stitch ¼" (6 mm) seam. Turn right side out; press. Topstitch both seams.

6) Staystitch the outer fabric and lining pieces for flap/back/divider for 1" (2.5 cm) at marks for flap foldline, ¼" (6 mm) from edge; clip to stitching at marks.

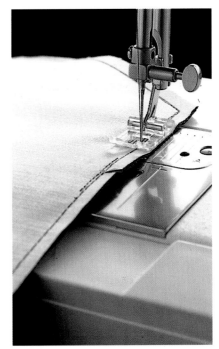

7) Pin purse flap to lining, right sides together; stitch around flap in ¼" (6 mm) seam, beginning and ending stitching at clips.

8) Stitch remaining side of zipper to flap/back/divider at end opposite the flap, as in step 4. Turn right side out; press. Topstitch seam.

9) Press tab strip in half lengthwise, wrong sides together. Open, and press raw edges to the center crease, wrong sides together; refold at the original crease.

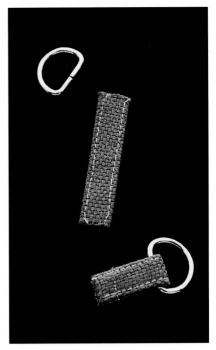

10) Stitch close to folded edges of tab strip. Cut two 2" (5 cm) pieces from strip. Insert one piece into D-ring; stitch ends together. Repeat for remaining piece.

(Continued on next page)

How to Sew a Clutch Purse (continued)

11) Fold purse at zipper, with outer fabrics together. Mark stitching lines for zippered divider 6" (15 cm) below zipper and 1½" (3.8 cm) from sides. Insert one tab at each side, ½" (1.3 cm) below zipper. Stitch on marked lines through all layers, catching tabs in stitching.

12) Pin sides of front/divider, right sides together, matching edges; do not pin through flap/back/divider. Stitch ¼" (6 mm) seam; finish the seam allowances. Turn right side out.

13) Fold the flap/back/divider, right sides together, matching clipped edge to top of divider; pin at sides. Stitch ¼" (6 mm) seam; finish the seam allowances. Turn purse right side out; press.

14) Edgestitch around flap and back section of purse, catching lining in stitching at bottom. Edgestitch purse front at sides and bottom. Secure the snap to the flap and purse front. Attach chain shoulder strap to D-rings, using self-closing clasps.

Tips for Punchneedle Embroidery

Position fabric drum-tight in an embroidery hoop that is slightly larger than the design. Retighten the fabric in the hoop, if necessary, while stitching.

Use machine embroidery threads directly from the spool to eliminate frequent rethreading of the punchneedle.

Make a test sample to determine the density of the pile and the spacing between the rows of stitching.

Experiment with the different punchneedle depth gauges to vary the pile depth.

Allow the thread to feed freely into the punchneedle without any drag or tension.

Do not reuse thread if it is necessary to remove stitches. Once thread has been looped, it will not feed properly through the needle a second time.

How to Stitch a Punchneedle Embroidery Design

1) Mark or transfer embroidery design on wrong side of fabric. Position fabric, wrong side up, over embroidery hoop; secure outer ring. Using a long needle threader, feed the thread through shaft of punchneedle. Feed the thread through eye of needle, threading from angled, open side through eye.

2) Decide on direction of stitching; hold needle at 90° angle to the fabric with angled, open side of the needle facing in that direction. Insert needle from wrong side of fabric until it is stopped by the depth gauge (arrow).

3) Lift needle to fabric surface, and just scratching the surface, move the needle forward about 1/16" (1.5 mm). Continue stitching, outlining the design area for first color. Work fill-in stitches by stitching rows back and forth.

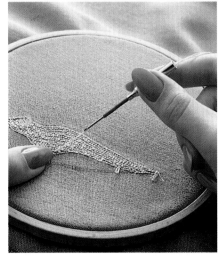

4) End stitching by grasping needle and fabric; gently pull needle out of fabric, allowing thread to slide through needle.

5) Stitch punchneedle design in any remaining colors. Clip thread tails on the wrong side of the fabric. Apply fabric glue to the back of the punchneedle design.

Tote Bags

Tote bags are handy for many occasions. Make several in a variety of fabrics for both casual and career wear. For organization, add pockets as desired to the front, back, and sides of this lined tote bag. A zippered pocket can be added to the lining.

Use a 90" (229 cm) length of webbing for the short handles shown above. If you prefer a bag with shoulder straps, use a 108" (275 cm) length of webbing.

YOU WILL NEED

¾ yd. (0.7 m) outer fabric.

1 yd. (0.95 m) lining fabric.

2½ yd. (2.3 m) webbing, 1" (2.5 cm) wide, for short handles; or 3 yd. (2.75 m) for shoulder straps.

⅛ yd. (0.15 m) fusible interfacing.

9" (23 cm) zipper, for optional lining pocket.

Pockets provide extra storage. Creative outer pockets (above) change the look of a basic tote. A zippered lining pocket (below) safeguards small items.

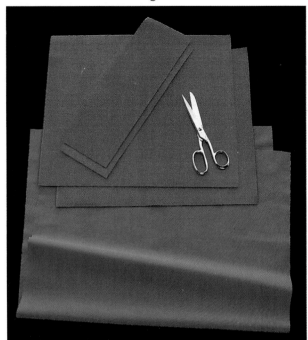

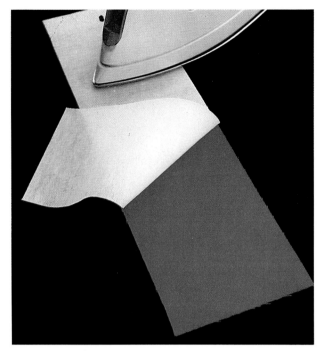

1) Cut one 19½" × 30½" (49.8 × 77.3 cm) lining piece. From outer fabric, cut two 13½" × 15½" (34.3 × 39.3 cm) pieces for bag front and back; cut two 4½" × 13½" (11.5 × 34.3 cm) pieces for side panels.

2) Cut one 4½" × 15½" (11.5 × 39.3 cm) piece for bottom of bag from outer fabric; cut one from interfacing. Fuse interfacing to bottom of bag on wrong side.

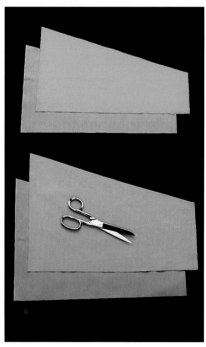

3) Determine the size and shape of pockets. For each pocket, cut one pocket and one lining piece, with width of pieces equal to cut width of bag front, back, or side panel; add ¼" (6 mm) seam allowances at upper and lower edges.

4) Place pocket and lining right sides together; stitch ¼" (6 mm) seam at upper edge. Clip seam allowances; turn pocket right side out. Press pocket, and edgestitch upper edge. Glue-baste edges to sides and lower edge of bag piece.

5) Pin bag front to bottom of bag, right sides together, matching long edges; stitch ¼" (6 mm) seam, beginning and ending stitching ¼" (6 mm) from ends. Repeat for back piece. Press seam allowances toward bottom of bag.

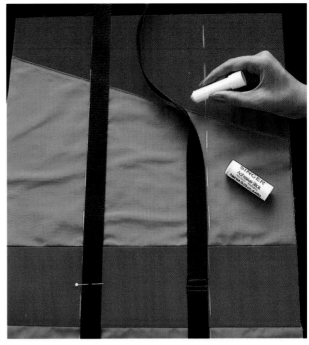

6) Mark lines on right side of pieced bag section 4½" (11.5 cm) from long edges, using chalk. Fold webbing in half, and pin-mark. Stitch ends of strap together in ½" (1.3 cm) seam; press open, and topstitch. Trim to ¼" (6 mm).

7) Glue-baste wrong side of strap to right side of bag, placing outer edge of webbing on marked line and centering seam and pin mark on bottom of bag.

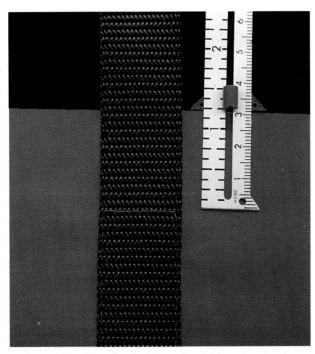

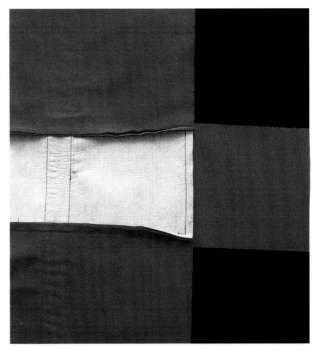

8) Topstitch along both sides of webbing, beginning and ending stitching 1¼" (3.2 cm) from the upper edges of the bag.

9) Pin lower edge of one side panel to bottom of bag, right sides together. With bottom of bag facing up, stitch ¼" (6 mm) seam, beginning and ending at previous seamlines; do not catch seam allowances in stitching. Repeat for remaining side panel.

(Continued on next page)

How to Sew a Tote Bag (continued)

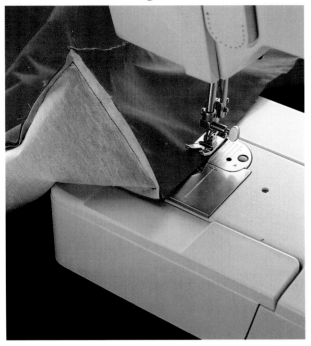

10) Pin side panels to bag front and back, matching raw edges. Stitch ¼" (6 mm) seams, ending at previous seamline; do not catch seam allowances in stitching.

11) Insert lining pocket, opposite, if desired. Fold lining in half crosswise, right sides together. Stitch ¼" (6 mm) seams on the sides, leaving 6" (15 cm) opening in one seam. Press seam allowances open.

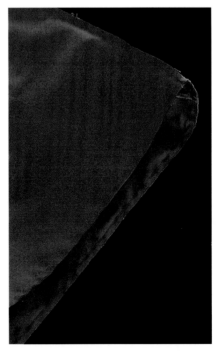

12) Stitch about 4" (10 cm) across corner; trim to ¼" (6 mm) seam allowance. Repeat for opposite side.

13) Pin bag to lining, with right sides together and raw edges even; center the lining seams on side panels. Stitch ¼" (6 mm) seam at upper edge; do not catch webbing in stitching.

14) Turn bag right side out through opening in side seam of lining; machine-stitch opening closed. Press upper edge of bag; edgestitch. Secure the webbing to the upper edge of the bag as shown, stitching through all layers.

How to Apply a Zippered Lining Pocket

1) **Cut** 2" × 10" (5 × 25.5 cm) piece of nonwoven sew-in interfacing; mark ¼" × 9" (6 mm × 23 cm) rectangle, centered on interfacing. Place interfacing 3" (7.5 cm) from one short end of lining, on right side. Stitch on marked lines, using short stitch length. Slash through layers at center of rectangle, clipping diagonally to corners.

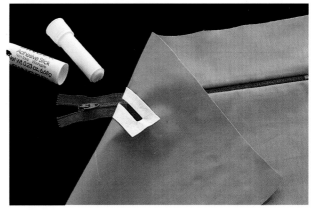

2) **Turn** interfacing to wrong side of lining along stitching; press. Trim interfacing to within ½" (1.3 cm) of stitching. Center zipper under opening, right sides up; glue-baste in place. Cut 10" × 16" (25.5 × 40.5 cm) pocket piece.

3) **Glue-baste** one short end of pocket piece to lower edge of zipper tape, matching edges; pocket piece will extend above raw edge of lining.

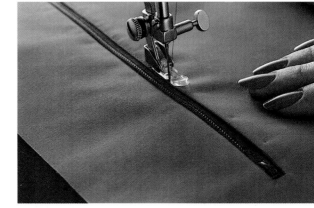

4) **Edgestitch** lower edge of opening, from right side, securing zipper tape; do not stitch beyond the ends of the opening.

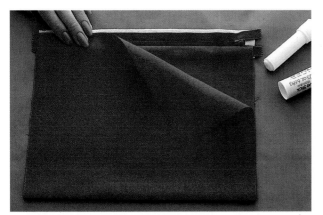

5) **Fold** pocket piece down; press. Glue-baste the remaining short end of pocket piece to upper edge of zipper tape, matching edges.

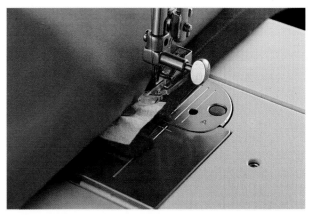

6) **Turn** lining over. From right side, fold lining to expose side of pocket. Using zipper foot, stitch ½" (1.3 cm) seam at side of pocket, stitching through the triangle. Repeat for the opposite side. Complete edgestitching around zipper opening, from right side.

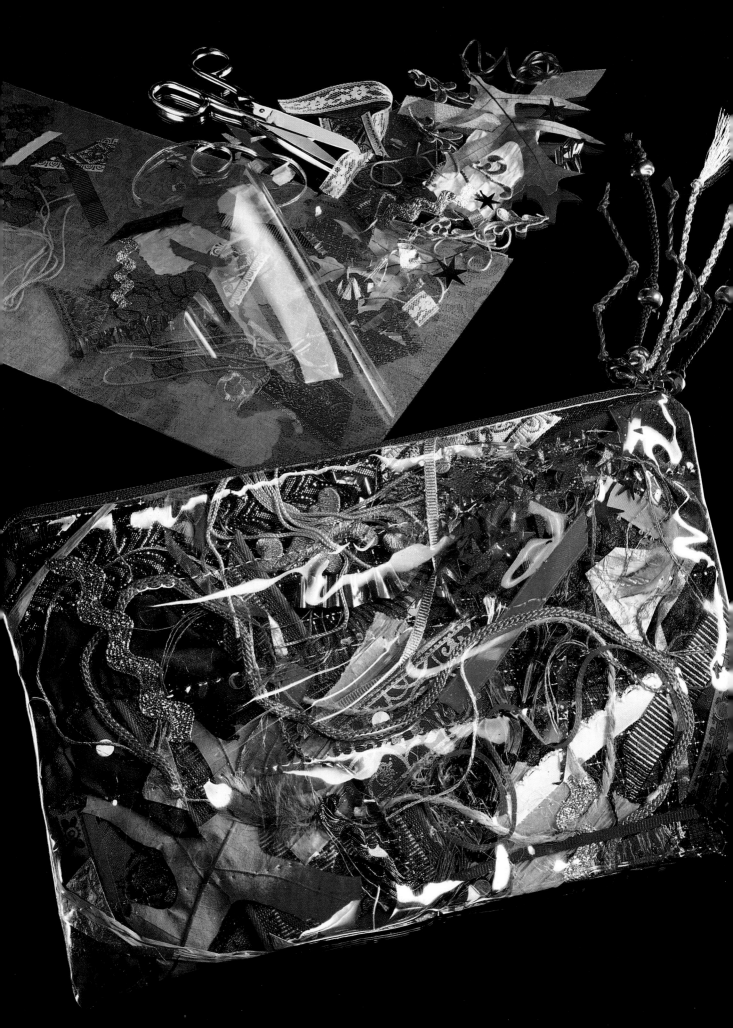

Confetti Bags

Bits of fabrics and trims, sandwiched between a foundation fabric and clear vinyl, make clutches and totes eye-catching. These zippered bags can be sewn in many sizes. Easy methods make confetti bags quick to construct; simple box corners and topstitched handles are added to the tote bag.

Create the confetti from a grouping of fabrics, trims, and threads in related colors. For a variety of textures, include fabrics like velvets, satins, metallics, netting, and mesh. Use notions such as lace, rickrack, ribbon,

and seam binding. Feathers, glitter, metallic paper, and other nonsewing items are also suitable; use any relatively flat item that can be stitched through. The confetti can be applied sparingly, to allow the foundation fabric to show through, or it can be applied in a dense layer.

Use a 90/14 sewing machine needle. When stitching on the vinyl, use a long stitch length. Lubricate the bottom of the presser foot, if necessary, with a silicone lubricant.

YOU WILL NEED

Fabric for foundation.

Clear vinyl, 7-gauge for small bags or 8-gauge for large bags.

Lining fabric, optional.

Fabric scraps and trims; additional embellishments as desired.

Decorative cording or ribbon, and beads, for tassel.

Zipper, at least ½" (1.3 cm) longer than the width of the bag.

Webbing and leather or synthetic suede scraps, for tote bags.

Spray adhesive; glue stick.

Bits of fabrics and trims give a whimsical look to these clutches and totes. Shown here are regular and billfold-size clutches, and a generous tote bag.

How to Sew a Confetti Clutch

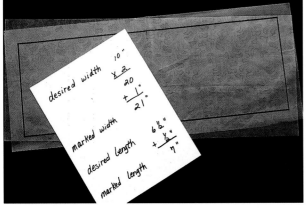

1) Determine desired width and length, or height, of bag. On vinyl, mark a rectangle twice the width of bag plus 1" (2.5 cm) by the length of the bag plus ½" (1.3 cm). Cut vinyl 1" (2.5 cm) outside marked lines. Cut foundation fabric to same size as vinyl.

2) Cut fabrics, trims, threads, and additional items into various shapes and sizes. Apply a light layer of spray adhesive to right side of foundation fabric. Position larger items on foundation, overlapping them as desired.

3) Layer smaller items on foundation, overlapping them as desired; respray lightly with adhesive as necessary to hold items in place.

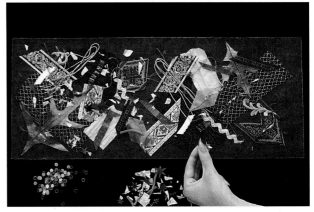

4) Sprinkle a top accent layer of items, such as glitter, sequins, and small bits of decorative thread, over previous layers.

5) Position the vinyl over the confetti fabric, matching edges. Stitch ⅛" (3 mm) inside marked lines; cut on marked lines. Stitch additional rows across the fabric, spacing rows about 1½" (3.8 cm) apart.

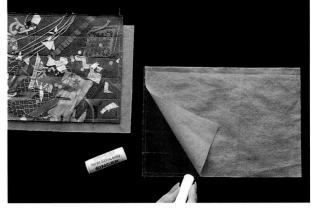

6) Cut confetti fabric in half to make purse front and back; stitch close to raw edges. If lining is desired, cut two lining pieces; glue-baste each piece to confetti fabric within ¼" (6 mm) seam allowances, wrong sides together. Finish raw edges.

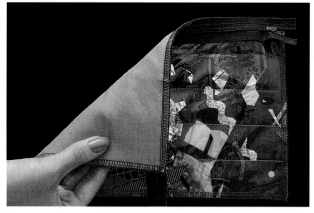

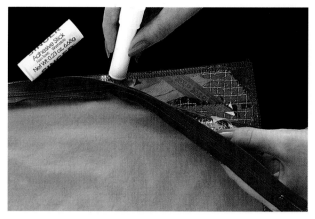

7) Glue-baste closed zipper to the upper edge of one piece, right sides together, aligning the edge of the piece to edge of zipper tape; ends of the zipper may extend beyond fabric. Stitch ¼" (6 mm) seam, using zipper foot.

8) Align the remaining piece to the zipper, right sides together, and stitch as in step 7. Partially open the zipper.

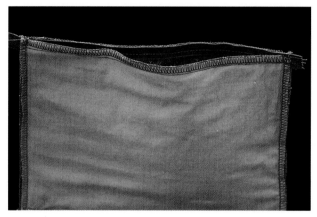

9) Fold fabric in half, right sides together. Stitch ¼" (6 mm) seams at sides and bottom. Trim ends of zipper even with edges of fabric. Turn bag right side out.

10) Cut three 12" to 16" (30.5 to 40.5 cm) strands of cording or ribbon; attach to zipper pull. Knot cords and add beads as desired.

How to Sew a Confetti Tote Bag

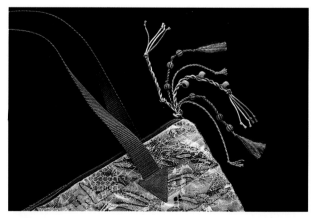

1) Make bag, following steps 1 to 9, opposite. Stitch box corners, if desired, stitching 3" to 4" (7.5 to 10 cm) across corners, before turning bag right side out.

2) Cut two pieces of webbing, for handles, to desired length. Position handles on each side of bag; glue-baste. Stitch across ends of webbing. Cut leather or suede into four patches; glue-baste over ends of webbing. Edgestitch around patches. Add tassel as in step 10.

Scarves
& Ties

Scarves

Scarves are versatile fashion accents that are easy to make. Depending on the fabric selection, they can accessorize any style, from casual to dressy.

Fabric Selection

The most important consideration in selecting fabric for a scarf is that it be drapable. Soft, silky fabrics drape well and tie easily. Challis is also suitable for scarves, but because it has a tendency to be bulky, it should be used for simple ties or wraps. Lightweight cottons are attractive for scarves with a casual look. For dressier scarves, use fabrics such as silk charmeuse, chiffons, and metallics.

Scarf Measurements

Scarves can be made in any size. Basic square scarves range in size from 30" to 45" (76 to 115 cm). Large square scarves, to be worn as shawls, range from 54" to 60" (137 to 152.5 cm). Rectangular scarves range in width from 4" to 11" (10 to 28 cm) and are generally 45" to 72" (115 to 183 cm) long.

For the most attractive look, make scarves that are in proportion to your body size. You may want to measure some of your favorite scarves to determine the sizes that are the most flattering.

When making scarves, it is important to cut the fabric precisely on the grainline. Pull the crosswise and lengthwise threads at the desired measurements, and cut along the pulled threads.

Edge Finishes

There are several ways to finish the edges of scarves. Fringed edges are a simple decorative finish, suitable for scarves made from stable fabrics. A narrow machine-stitched hem is an easy-to-sew edge finish, suitable for all scarf fabrics. Hand-rolled hems are an elegant couture finish for natural fabrics. An overlock rolled hem, stitched on a serger, is a quick edge finish that simulates a hand-rolled hem; the 3-thread rolled hem works best for most fabrics, but a 2-thread rolled hem is more appropriate for chiffons and other lightweight fabrics. Rectangular scarves are often hemmed at the sides and fringed at the ends.

YOU WILL NEED

Fabric.
Lightweight thread.
Embellishments, if desired.

Edge finishes for scarves include (left to right) fringed edges, narrow machine-stitched hems, hand-rolled hems, and overlock rolled hems.

How to Sew a Scarf with a Fringed Edge Finish

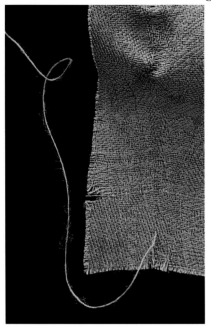

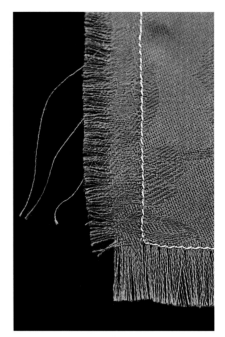

1) **Measure** desired fringe width from each cut edge; mark with a clip. Pull a thread along each edge at clip marks.

2) **Stitch** around scarf, if desired, on pulled-thread lines, pivoting at corners. Stitching helps prevent fabric from fraying; it is not necessary for tightly woven fabrics.

3) **Remove** threads, one by one, up to stitching.

How to Sew a Scarf with a Narrow Machine-stitched Hem

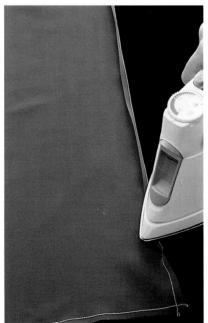

1) **Machine-stitch** ¼" (6 mm) from the fabric edges, using lightweight thread. Fold one edge to wrong side on stitching line; press fold.

2) **Stitch** close to fold, using short stitch length. Trim excess fabric close to stitching, using appliqué scissors.

3) **Fold** the hem edge to the wrong side, enclosing raw edge. Machine-stitch an even distance from edge. Repeat for remaining edges.

How to Sew a Scarf with a Hand-rolled Hem

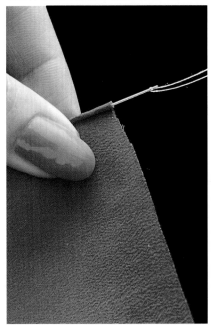

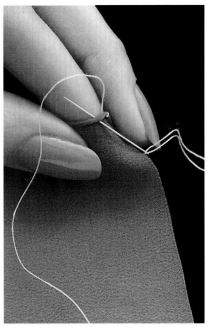

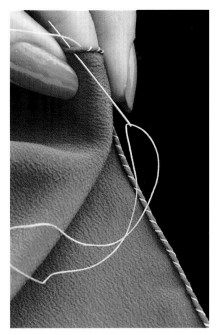

1) Thread needle with single strand of waxed lightweight thread; knot end. Moisten thumb and forefinger; position needle at edge of fabric, and roll fabric a scant ¼" (6 mm) around needle. Remove needle.

2) Insert the needle under the roll and out through top of roll. Stitch, holding fabric taut, as shown, and keeping needle at 45° angle; space stitches about ⅛" (3 mm) apart.

3) Continue rolling edge of fabric with fingers and stitching roll in place. Thread should encircle the roll on wrong side.

How to Sew a Scarf with an Overlock Rolled Hem

1) Adjust overlock machine for a 3-thread or 2-thread rolled hem stitch. Stitch one side, holding the fabric taut and trimming the edge with knives; hold tail chain at beginning of hem, and leave a 4" (10 cm) tail chain at end.

2) Reposition next edge of scarf under presser foot. Stitch, holding tail chain at beginning of hem so fabric remains taut and square at corner. Repeat for remaining edges.

3) Apply liquid fray preventer to corners; allow to dry. Trim tail chains.

Embellishing Scarves

For a distinctive look, you may add beaded dangles to the corner of a scarf, embellish narrow hems with beaded edging, or apply sequins or textile paints to create a design.

To save time, confine beadwork and sequins to small areas, adding a beaded edging to just the ends of a rectangular scarf or applying sequins in scattered designs. When embellishing a scarf with beads, make sure the fabric and the hem edge can support the weight of the beads; seed beads are recommended for edging.

Use metallic textile paints to add sparkle to a scarf fabric. Apply the paints sparingly to prevent the fabric from becoming stiff; a fan brush works well for this purpose. Test the paint on a small scrap of the fabric, thinning it, if necessary, with an extender.

Sequins, applied in a scattered design, dress up a simple crepe or chiffon scarf.

Beaded dangles, stitched to the corners of a challis scarf, add a touch of sophistication.

How to Apply Sequins

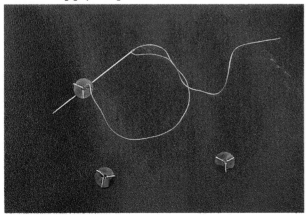

Thread needle with a single strand of lightweight thread. Secure thread on right side of fabric. Take stitch up through center of sequin and down at edge of sequin; repeat for two more stitches, spacing them at equal distances around sequin. Secure the thread under the sequin.

How to Apply Beaded Dangles

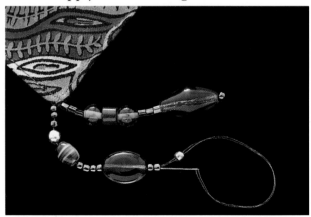

Thread beading needle with double strand of waxed cotton-wrapped polyester thread. Bring needle up at corner of fabric and through several beads. Then add a final bead, called the *stop*. Bring needle back through all beads except the stop. Knot thread on wrong side of scarf after each dangle stitch.

Beaded edging adds sparkle to a silk jacquard scarf.

Metallic textile paint highlights a silk twill scarf.

How to Apply Beaded Edging

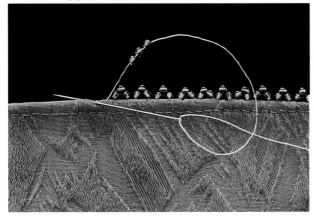

Thread beading needle with a single strand of waxed cotton-wrapped polyester thread. Bring needle up at edge of fabric and through three seed beads. Take a short stitch in edge of fabric so third bead lies next to first bead and so second bead is raised away from fabric. Take next stitch close to previous stitch.

How to Apply Metallic Textile Paint

Tape scarf fabric taut to work surface; place a sheet of paper under sheer fabric to absorb any excess paint. Using metallic textile paint and synthetic fan brush, paint design, applying light pressure. Heat-set paint according to the manufacturer's directions.

Soft turtleneck effect is created with the folding method on page 60. This technique works best on large square scarves.

Bias-draped effect is achieved by folding a square scarf. The scarf shown here is knotted in the back, but for another look, the scarf may be knotted at one side, as shown on page 60.

Ways to Wear Square Scarves

Square scarves can be draped softly at the neckline in a number of ways. Vary the effect by folding and tying them creatively, and experiment with placing the knot at the back, side, or front.

For more versatility, try wearing a large square scarf, tied sarong-style, adding flair to a dressy pants outfit. Or tie the scarf as a blouson shawl for a dramatic evening accessory.

Shawls can be created from large square scarves. For a blouson shawl (left), drape the scarf across your back; then tie the corners together at each side. For a shoulder wrap (right), fold the scarf into a triangle, and drape it over one shoulder; knot the scarf at the waist or tuck the ends under a belt.

Traditional ascot is created with a square scarf that has been double-folded into a rectangle. Place the scarf around the neck, and flip one end of the scarf over the other.

Pleated ascot is created with a square scarf, folded into accordion-style pleats. Place the pleated scarf around the neck, and flip one end of the scarf over the other, fanning out the pleats.

Classic headwrap is made with a square scarf folded into a triangle. Bring the ends of the scarf to the back, and tie the scarf over the points of the triangle.

Sarong-style waist accent is simply a square scarf with beaded dangles at the corners. It is folded on the diagonal, then draped and knotted around the waist.

Slipknot (page 61) provides an easy way to neatly tie a rectangular scarf.

Ways to Wear Rectangular Scarves

Whether draped softly around the neck or tied in a simple bow, a rectangular scarf is versatile to wear. Secured at the neckline with a jewelry pin, it adds a dramatic finishing touch to a basic blouse or dress.

A long rectangular scarf, worn as a belt, adds style to a silky pants outfit. Wear it twisted and knotted around the waist. Or tie it at the waistline in a slipknot or half bow.

Bow effect is surprisingly easy to achieve, following the instructions on page 61.

Cowl effect is achieved by draping a rectangular scarf around your neck with the center of the scarf in front. Crisscross the scarf in the back, bringing the ends around to the front.

Looped scarf is created by folding a rectangular scarf in half crosswise; place the scarf around your neck, pulling the ends through the center fold.

Half bow (page 61) is similar to the slipknot and creates a dramatic look with a rectangular scarf.

How to Tie a Square Scarf for a Soft Turtleneck Effect

1) Fold square scarf into a triangle. Position scarf around neck, with points of triangle in front.

2) Wrap ends of scarf around neck; crisscross them in back. Knot in front.

3) Pull folded edge of fabric down over the knot; arrange the folds.

How to Tie a Square Scarf for a Bias-draped Effect

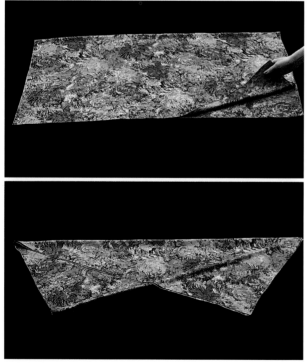

1) Fold square scarf into a rectangle (top). Grasp opposite corners, forming double points (bottom).

2) Tie scarf around neck, with knot placed at one side as shown here, or knotted at the back as shown on page 56. Arrange the folds.

How to Tie a Rectangular Scarf for a Bow Effect

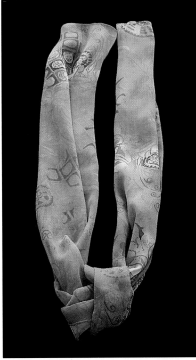

1) Tie a loose knot in the center of a rectangular scarf.

2) Drape scarf around neck with knot in front; crisscross ends of scarf in back, bringing them around to the front.

3) Insert ends through the front of the knot in opposite directions.

How to Tie a Rectangular Scarf in a Slipknot

Tie a loose knot in one end of a rectangular scarf. Insert other end down through front of knot; tighten knot as desired, and arrange folds so ends flare out.

How to Tie a Rectangular Scarf in a Half Bow

Tie a loose knot in one end of a rectangular scarf. Fold opposite end in half, forming a loop; insert loop up through the front of the knot. Tighten knot as desired, and arrange folds so ends flare out.

Hand-dyed Silk Scarves

Hand-dye silk using the salt technique to create your own designer scarves. Dyed silk may also be used for other fashion accessories, such as ties (page 66), ponytail wraps (page 78), and fabric-wrapped bracelets (page 119).

The salt technique for dyeing silk is easy and creates dramatic results. First, the dye is applied to silk that has been stretched over a frame. Then salt is applied to the damp fabric; the salt attracts and absorbs the dye in the immediate area, creating a mottled effect.

Use white silk, such as China silk, pongee, or satin, in the desired weight. Most silk yardage is 40" to 45" (102 to 115 cm) wide, but the usable width may be narrower after the dyeing process. Before dyeing the fabric, wash it, using mild soap, to remove the sizing, and hang it to dry.

To maintain the drapability of the fabric, apply silk dyes; avoid using silk paints, which stiffen the fabric. Silk dyes are water-based, and colors of the same brand may be mixed together. Some silk dyes are mixed with a chemical water; others require no mixing and can be used directly from the concentrated dye. Dyes can be diluted with water to create pastels.

When dyeing silk, work in a well-ventilated room and wear rubber gloves. Protect the entire work area with plastic, and place newsprint over the plastic in the mixing and dyeing areas to absorb any spills. Mix and measure dyes in containers that will not be used for food purposes.

Before starting a project, experiment on small pieces of fabric to see how the silk dyes react. For the most dramatic effects, use concentrated dyes in dark, rich colors, such as deep blues and reds. The dyes spread quickly, wicking one color into the next, and blending will occur. The colors in the damp fabric will appear much more intense than in the finished project.

For maximum color retention, heat-set the dyes using the steam method on page 65. The dyes may also be set using a chemical fixative recommended by the dye manufacturer. Depending on the product used, either the chemical fixative is painted on the fabric, or the fabric is rinsed in a chemical bath.

YOU WILL NEED

Silk fabric.
2 × 4 boards for frame; silk tacks or push pins.
Silk dyes; chemical fixative, optional.
Silk salt or rock salt.
Synthrapol®, or a mild soap.
Bristled brushes or sponge brushes, for applying dye.
Wide, soft-bristled brush for removing the salt from the fabric.
Rubber gloves.
Plastic sheets; newsprint.

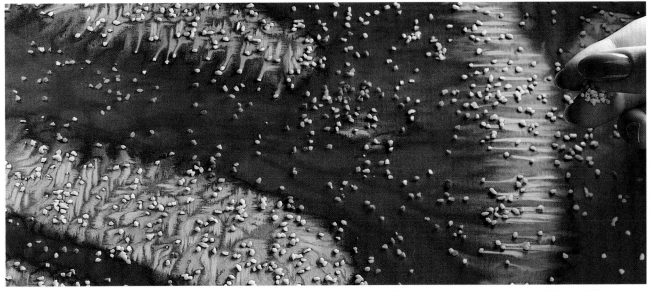

The salt technique is used to create a mottled effect in hand-dyed silk. Salt is sprinkled on the fabric while it is still damp from the dyes. The salt attracts and absorbs the dyes, spreading and blending the colors into unique patterns.

How to Hand-dye Silk Using the Salt Technique

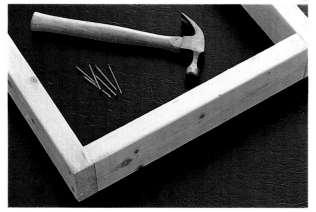

1) Make frame by nailing together 2 × 4 boards, cut to desired frame size, positioning the boards so frame is 3½" (9 cm) high.

2) Tack the silk fabric to one side of frame, using silk tacks or push pins. Stretch the fabric taut; secure on opposite side. If silk dyes require any preparation, follow manufacturer's directions.

3a) Striped design. Apply dyes, using brush; begin at one end, applying stripes of color that overlap. Work quickly, and adjust fabric as necessary to keep it taut.

3b) Random design. Apply dyes, using brush; apply one color in several places, repeating with additional colors as desired. Work quickly, and adjust fabric as necessary to keep it taut.

4) Sprinkle salt on damp fabric. For clear definitions, apply salt sparingly; if salt falls heavily in an area, remove excess. Leave salt in place until the fabric is completely dry; wicking process starts in about 10 minutes and continues until fabric is dry.

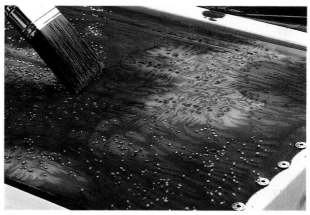

5) Brush salt from fabric, using a wide, soft-bristled brush; dispose of salt. Remove fabric from frame. Heat-set dyes using steam method (opposite); or set the dyes using a chemical fixative according to the manufacturer's directions.

6) Allow dyes to set at least 24 hours. Rinse fabric in cool water until water runs clear; continue rinsing fabric, gradually raising the water temperature until warm water runs clear.

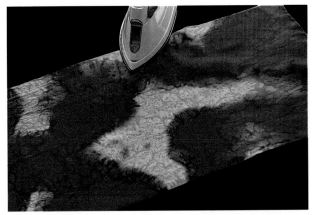

7) Hand wash fabric in warm water, using a mild soap. Hang to dry; iron while damp. Make scarf as desired (pages 51 to 55).

How to Heat-set Dyes Using the Steam Method

1) Place three sheets of unprinted newsprint on each side of hand-dyed silk fabric. Fold and roll paper and fabric together into a loose bundle; tie or tape the bundle in place.

2) Pour 2 to 3 c. (474 to 711 mL) of water in a large kettle that contains a rack. Place bundle on the rack; do not allow bundle to touch water. Shape a dome of aluminum foil; place over bundle.

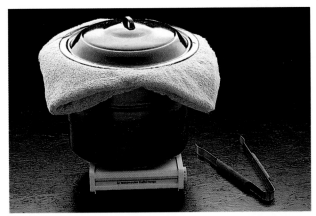

3) Place a towel over pan to absorb excess moisture; place lid on pan. On burner, steam the bundle for 30 minutes; turn bundle over after 15 minutes. The steam must rise and penetrate the fabric, without getting fabric wet.

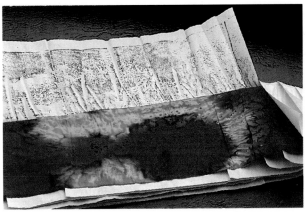

4) Unwrap bundle; hang fabric to dry, taking care that damp fabric layers do not touch.

Ties

For a soft menswear look, wear a bias-cut reversible tie in a loose knot. Make a variety of ties to wear with your favorite shirts.

To turn a tie into a one-of-a-kind accessory, embellish it with beads or couching (page 23), or with an appliqué. Or create a collage effect on the tie by adding patches of fabric and leather. If the tie will be embellished with couching or a collage, apply the embellishments to the interfaced tie fabric before you stitch it to the lining.

This tie has rounded corners for a more feminine look. It is made using a simple stitch-and-turn method. Choose lightweight to mediumweight fabrics and a soft woven interfacing. If you plan to embellish the tie, choose a firmer fabric, such as a linen or raw silk, for the embellished side.

YOU WILL NEED

⅝ yd. (0.6 m) each of two fabrics.
⅝ yd. (0.6 m) soft sew-in woven interfacing.
Embellishments as desired.

Embellishments add a finishing touch to a simple tie. Beading (**a**) that complements the design of the fabric is hand-stitched in place. Couching (**b**) adds texture and design to a solid-colored fabric.

A collage (**c**) is created from patches of fabric and leather, edgestitched in place; the edges of the fabric patches are pressed under before stitching. A purchased appliqué (**d**) is applied to a tie using fusible web.

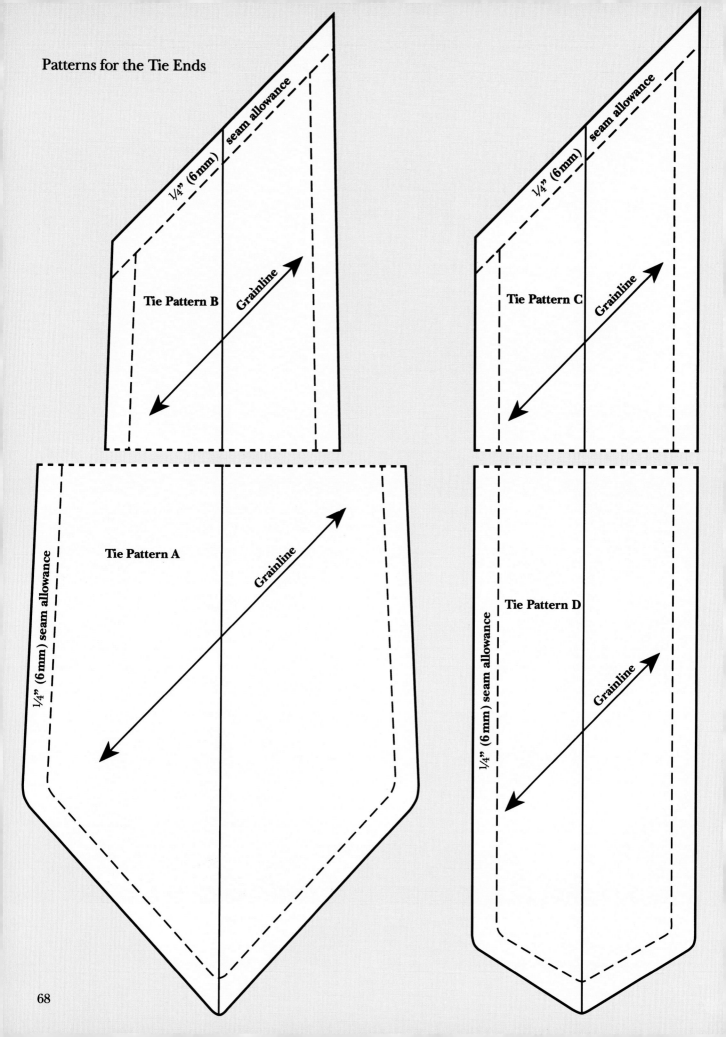

Patterns for the Tie Ends

Tie Pattern B

¼" (6 mm) seam allowance

Grainline

Tie Pattern C

¼" (6 mm) seam allowance

Grainline

Tie Pattern A

¼" (6 mm) seam allowance

Grainline

Tie Pattern D

¼" (6 mm) seam allowance

Grainline

How to Complete the Pattern Pieces for a Tie

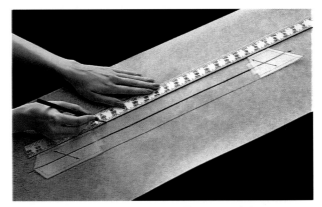

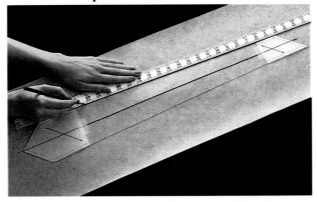

Pattern for wide end of tie. Trace partial patterns A and B, opposite, onto tracing paper. On another piece of tracing paper, draw 28" (71 cm) line. Align patterns as shown, placing center lines of patterns over marked line; center length of pattern should measure 27" (68.5 cm). Using straightedge, draw angled lines to connect sides of pattern.

Pattern for narrow end of tie. Trace partial patterns C and D, opposite, onto tracing paper. On another piece of tracing paper, draw a 25" (63.5 cm) line. Align patterns as shown, placing the center lines of patterns over marked line; center length of pattern should measure 24" (61 cm). Using straightedge, draw lines to connect sides of pattern.

How to Sew a Tie

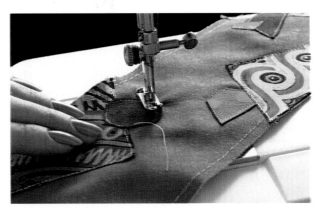

1) Cut one wide and one narrow end from tie fabric, lining, and interfacing, using completed patterns, above. For each fabric, stitch ends, right sides together, in ¼" (6 mm) seam. Press seam allowances open.

2) Place interfacing on wrong side of tie fabric; baste in place. If desired, embellish tie fabric with collage of fabric and suede or leather, as shown, or with couching (page 23).

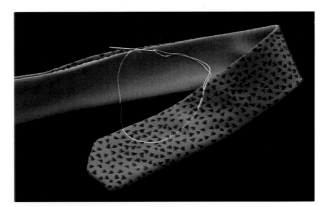

3) Place tie fabric and lining right sides together, matching raw edges. Stitch ¼" (6 mm) seam around tie, taking care not to stretch bias edges; leave 3" (7.5 cm) opening at center back of one seam. Trim corners.

4) Turn tie right side out through opening; press. Embellish tie fabric with beading (page 23) or a purchased appliqué, if desired, taking care not to catch lining with stitches. Slipstitch opening closed.

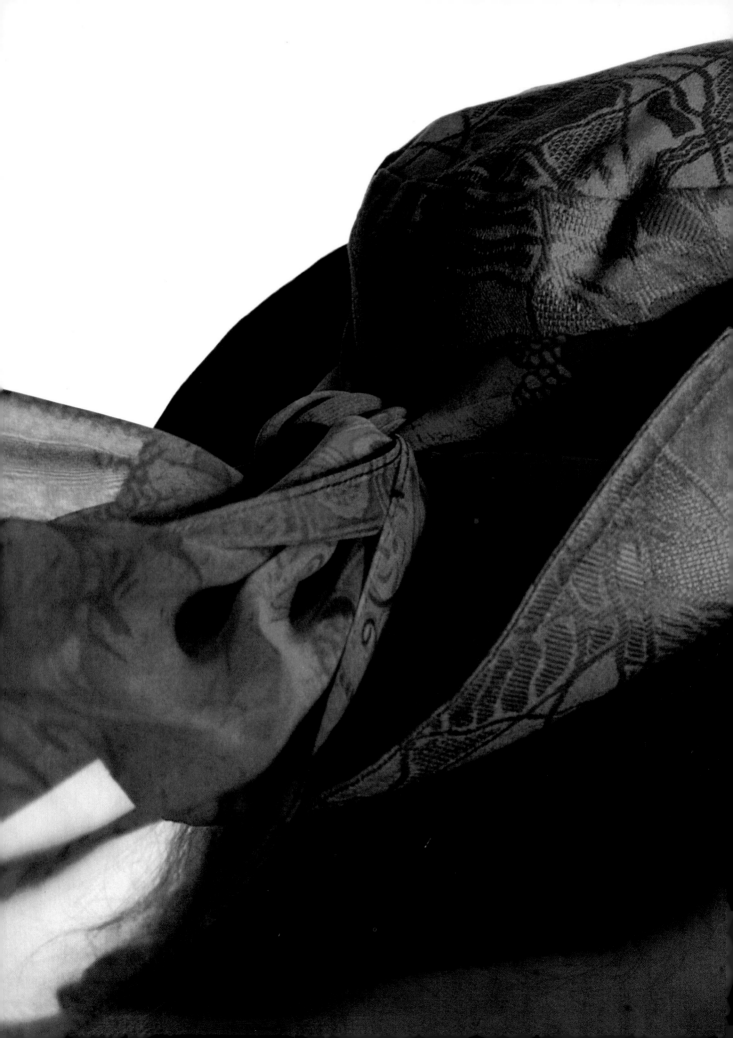

Hats & Hair Accessories

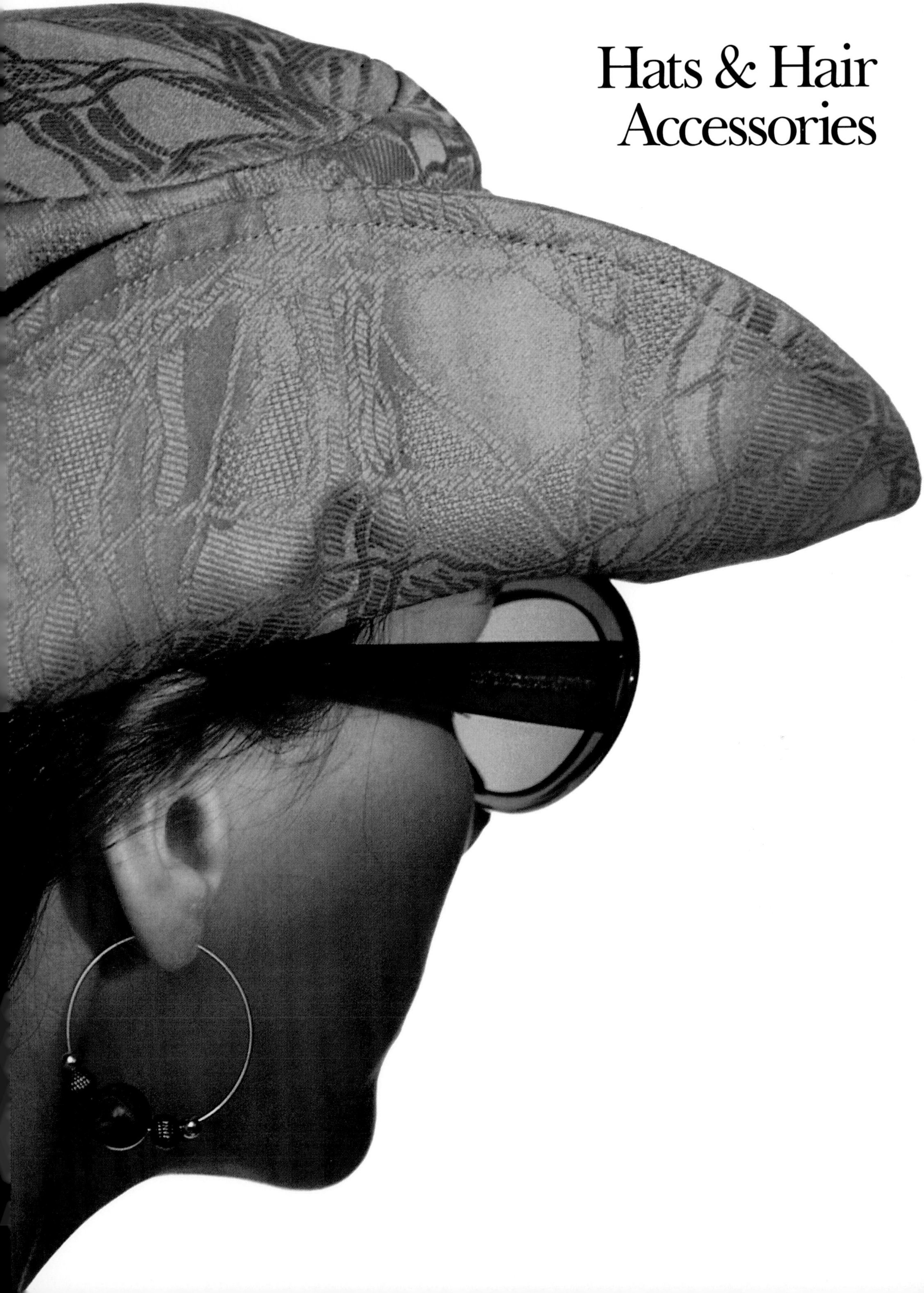

Hats

Enhance any outfit by adding a hat that can be styled for dressy or casual wear. This easy-to-sew lined hat is made using circular pattern pieces for the top and brim and a rectangular piece for the crown. Fusible knit interfacing gives the hat an unstructured look and allows it to be shaped and embellished in several ways.

Choose mediumweight fabrics, such as damasks, decorator prints, broadcloths, and some denims. When using a supple fabric, interface all the outer fabric pieces. When using a firm or crisp fabric, you may want to interface only the brim pieces. Preshrink the interfacing by rinsing it gently by hand in warm water; allow it to air dry. Or steam the interfacing, fusible side up, before applying it to the fabric.

Tie a scarf or trim around the crown as a hatband. Or add lace to the underside of the brim. Experiment with various ways to wear the hat, pinning the brim at the front or sides. Also try positioning the hat at several angles to find the most flattering style. Secure the brim with an artificial flower, a pin, or a button.

YOU WILL NEED

Outer fabric; ⅝ yd. (0.6 m) of 45" (115 cm) fabric, or ½ yd. (0.5 m) of 60" (152.5 cm) fabric.

¼ yd. (0.25 m) lining fabric.

1 yd. (0.95 m) fusible knit interfacing.

¾ yd. (0.7 m) grosgrain ribbon, 1" (2.5 cm) wide.

Embellishments as desired.

How to Make a Hat Pattern

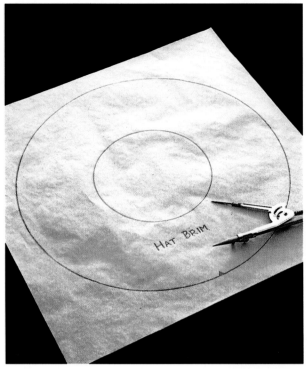

1) Draw 15" (38 cm) circle on tracing paper, using a compass, or pencil and string. Using same center point, draw 6½" (16.3 cm) circle. Label piece for hat brim; mark a notch on outer cutting line.

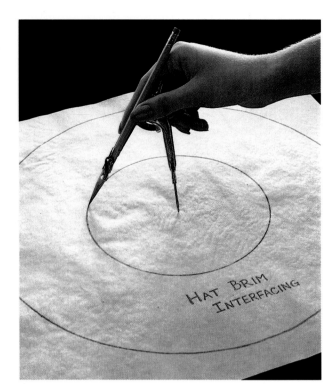

2) Draw 14½" (36.8 cm) circle. Using same center point, draw 7" (18 cm) circle. Label piece for hat brim interfacing.

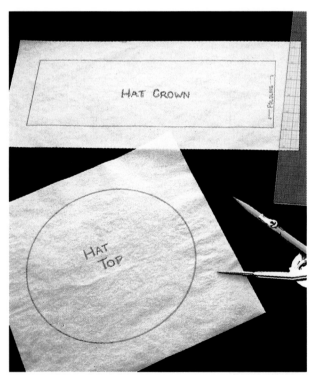

3) Draw 4" × 12" (10 × 30.5 cm) rectangle, and mark one short end for foldline; label for hat crown. Draw 7½" (19.3 cm) circle; label for hat top.

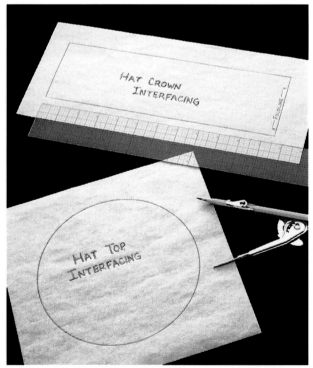

4) Draw interfacing patterns for crown and top, if interfacing is desired. Draw 3½" × 11¼" (9 × 28.7 cm) rectangle, and mark one short end for foldline; label for hat crown interfacing. Draw 7" (18 cm) circle; label for hat top interfacing.

How to Sew a Hat

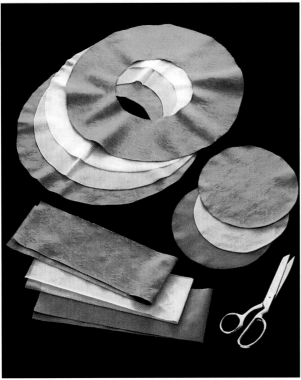

1) Make pattern (opposite). From outer fabric, cut two brims, one crown, and one top. From the lining fabric, cut one crown and one top. From interfacing, cut two brims, and, if desired, one crown and one top.

2) Fuse interfacing to wrong side of each hat piece cut from outer fabric, centering interfacing on fabric.

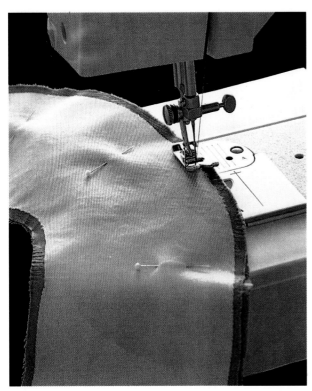

3) Pin brim pieces, right sides together, matching notch. Stitch ¼" (6 mm) seam around outer edge. Over a pressing ham, press seam open.

4) Turn brim right side out. Press seam edge. Topstitch ¼" (6 mm) from edge; press.

(Continued on next page)

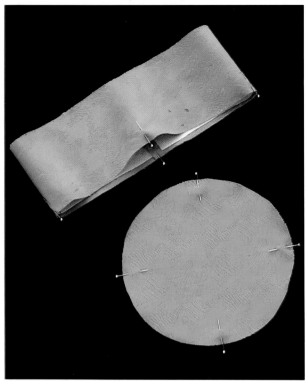

5) Fold crown, right sides together, matching short ends; stitch ¼" (6 mm) seam. Press seam open. Divide the upper edge of crown into fourths, and pin-mark; repeat for top.

6) Pin crown to top, right sides together, matching pin marks. Stitch ¼" (6 mm) seam. Over a pressing ham, press seam allowances toward crown.

7) Repeat steps 5 and 6 for lining pieces. Place lining inside hat, wrong sides together, matching seams; machine-baste ⅛" (3 mm) from lower edge of crown.

8) Divide brim into fourths, and pin-mark; repeat for lower edge of crown.

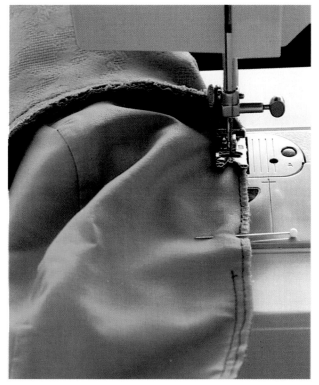

9) Pin lower edge of crown to the brim, right sides together, matching pin marks. Stitch ¼" (6 mm) seam, easing crown to fit brim.

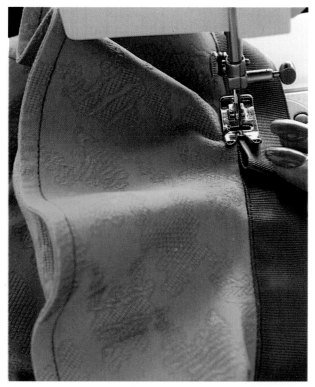

10) Stitch grosgrain ribbon to brim seam allowance, brim side up, so edge of ribbon just overlaps stitching line. Fold under ribbon at end of stitching, and overlap opposite end. Stitch ends of ribbon together.

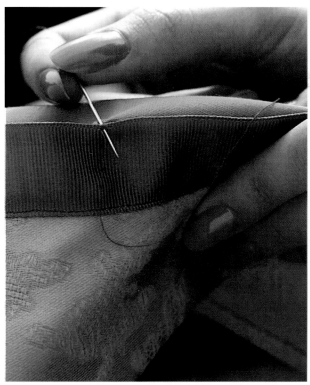

11) Hand-tack ribbon to hat lining at center front, center back, and sides.

12) Secure brim to crown at desired location; secure embellishment.

Ponytail Wraps

For ponytails, add a touch of color with simple-to-make elasticized ponytail wraps of grosgrain ribbon or fabric. The ribbon ponytail wraps are embellished with inserted trims like cording, decorative thread, or narrow ribbon.

When making ponytail wraps, vary the cut length of the strip according to the weight of the fabric or ribbon and the desired fullness. Generally, the length of the strip is about 30" (76 cm). A lightweight fabric, such as silk or chiffon, may be up to 36" (91.5 cm) in length. A shorter length may be used for heavier fabric or ribbon. Choose braided elastic of good quality for maximum stretch and recovery.

YOU WILL NEED

60" (152.5 cm) length of grosgrain ribbon, 1½" (3.8 cm) wide, and 3-yd. (2.75 cm) total length of desired trims, for ribbon ponytail wrap.

¼ yd. (0.25 m) fabric, for fabric ponytail wrap.

8" (20.5 cm) length of braided elastic, ¼" (6 mm) wide.

How to Sew a Ribbon Ponytail Wrap

1) Cut two 30" (76 cm) lengths of ribbon. Stitch ends of each ribbon strip together; stitch the ends of the elastic together. Cut desired trims into lengths ranging from 2" to 4" (5 to 10 cm).

2) Place the ribbons wrong sides together. Stitch ribbons together on outer edge, inserting trims to form overlapping loops as desired.

3) Insert elastic between ribbons. Stitch ribbons together along inner edge, bunching ribbon as you stitch. Do not catch elastic in stitching.

How to Sew a Fabric Ponytail Wrap

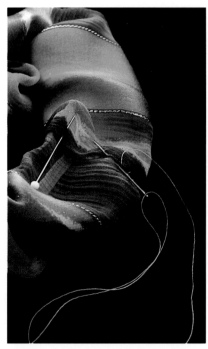

1) Cut 4½" (11.5 cm) strip of fabric to desired length. Fold fabric in half lengthwise, right sides together; stitch ¼" (6 mm) seam on long edge.

2) Turn fabric tube right side out. Insert elastic through tube; stitch elastic ends together securely.

3) Fold under ¼" (6 mm) on one end of fabric; lap over opposite end. Slipstitch; do not catch elastic in stitching.

Headbands

Use fabric scraps to make custom headbands. Inexpensive plastic headbands or plastic headband forms, available at fabric and craft stores, are easy to wrap with a bias-cut strip of fabric. If desired, the top of the headband may be padded with ¼" to ½" (6 mm to 1.3 cm) polyurethane foam. For a professional finish, gimp is glued to the inside of the headband.

For best results, use a firmly woven fabric; avoid slippery fabrics that are difficult to handle. Mediumweight to heavyweight fabrics are easier to wrap around headbands that have been padded with ½" (1.3 cm) polyurethane foam.

YOU WILL NEED

Fabric scraps.

Plastic headband form.

Polyurethane foam, ¼" to ½" (6 mm to 1.3 cm) thick, for a padded headband.

Spray adhesive, for a padded headband.

Thick craft glue.

½ **yd. (0.5 m) gimp.**

How to Make an Unpadded Headband

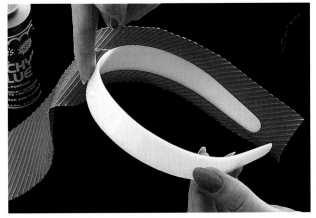

1) Cut a bias strip of fabric at least twice the width of the headband and about 2" (5 cm) longer. Spread a thin layer of glue on outside of the headband. Center headband on wrong side of fabric strip; secure.

2) Trim fabric so edges extend one-half the width of the headband; round fabric strip about ⅜" (1 cm) beyond ends of headband. Clip fabric at ends, and glue to inside of headband.

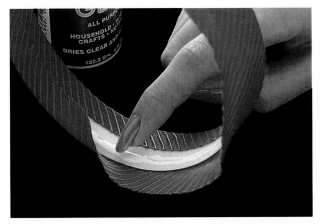

3) Glue one long edge of fabric to inside of headband, applying glue to the headband; work in sections, keeping fabric smooth. Repeat for opposite side.

4) Glue gimp, centering it on inside of headband and turning under ends.

How to Make a Padded Headband

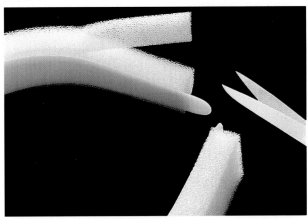

1) Spread a thin layer of glue on outside of headband; secure to strip of polyurethane foam. Cut foam even with edges of headband. If using ½" (1.3 cm) foam, trim foam ½" (1.3 cm) shorter than ends. Clamp ends of foam with clothespins until glue dries.

2) Follow steps 1 to 4 above, applying a light layer of spray adhesive to foam, to secure fabric; wrap the headband with fabric, pulling it taut to round the edges of the foam.

Embellishing Headbands

By embellishing headbands with trims, you can create a number of different styles. Depending on the look you want, combine dramatic fabrics with embellishments that sparkle, or use sportswear fabrics and sporty trims.

Most items can be glued in place, using a craft glue or hot glue. If trim will be wrapped around the headband, attach it before securing the gimp on the inside.

1) Twisted cording, applied in a diagonal wrap, is threaded with decorative beads to create a headband that is one of a kind.

2) Coordinating fabrics are wrapped in three or four separate sections. Wrap a decorative ribbon around the headband to conceal the raw edges where the fabric sections overlap.

3) Faceted stones highlight the fabric of this padded headband. For best results, secure the faceted stones with a gem glue.

4) Decorative ring embellishes a plain headband. Secure cording to the ring with larkspur knots, and glue in place. Wrap the ends of the headband with a narrow trim to conceal the ends of the cording.

5) Decorative buttons, glued in a row, provide a simple embellishment. Remove the shanks from the buttons, using a wire cutter.

6) Gold chain, woven with a narrow strip of synthetic suede or leather, adds a unique embellishment. Weave the suede or leather strip through the chain before gluing it in place.

Fabric-covered Barrettes

For a versatile selection of hair accessories, make barrettes in a variety of shapes and fabrics. For softness, pad the barrette with polyurethane foam. Then wrap it with bias-cut fabric for a smooth finish. Added accents like beads, pearls, or small decorative buttons may be applied to fabric-covered barrettes. Or for a dimensional effect, add a sheer ribbon, hand-stitching it in place along one edge.

Cover a purchased barrette, or cover a barrette base made from polymer clay, using one of the patterns below. A sheet of polymer clay, 3/16" (4.5 mm) thick, can be cut into any shape and baked to form a smooth, firm base; the clay base is rolled to this thickness in order for it to have adequate strength. Before working with the polymer clay, refer to the handling suggestions on page 95.

YOU WILL NEED

Fabric scraps.

Embellishments, such as sheer ribbon, pearls, or buttons, optional.

Purchased barrette; or polymer clay and spring barrette clip, about 3" (7.5 cm) long.

3/8 **yd. (0.35 m) gimp.**

Polyurethane foam, 1/4" (6 mm) thick.

Thick craft glue; spray adhesive.

Jewelry glue, mat knife, heavy-duty aluminum foil, and sandpaper, for polymer clay barrette.

Patterns for Polymer Clay Barrette Bases

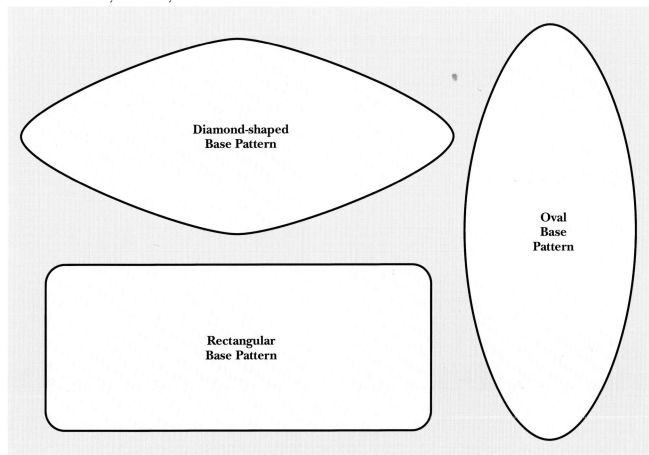

Diamond-shaped Base Pattern

Oval Base Pattern

Rectangular Base Pattern

How to Make a Polymer Clay Barrette Base

1) Roll polymer clay into sheet about 3/16" (4.5 mm) thick, using brayer or rolling pin. Trace the desired pattern (page 85) onto tracing paper; cut on marked line. Place pattern on clay; cut, using mat knife or paring knife.

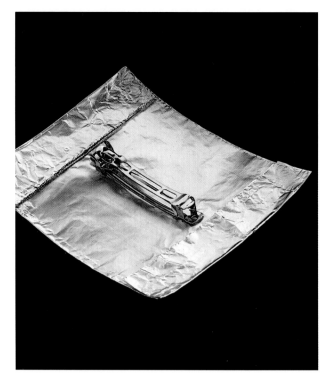

2) Fold a sheet of heavy-duty aluminum foil into thirds or fourths; folded sheet should be about 1" (2.5 cm) larger than clay design. Shape foil to match curve of barrette clip; fold the ends of the foil, if necessary, for support.

3) Place clay design on shaped foil; place on baking sheet, with barrette clip under foil for support. Bake in 225°F (107°C) preheated oven for 15 to 20 minutes. Allow clay to cool before removing it from foil.

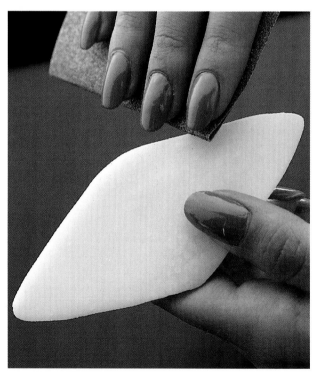

4) File edges of clay to bevel them, using sandpaper. Open barrette clip, and remove tension bar. Glue the barrette clip to back of curved clay piece, using jewelry glue. Replace tension bar.

How to Cover a Barrette with Fabric

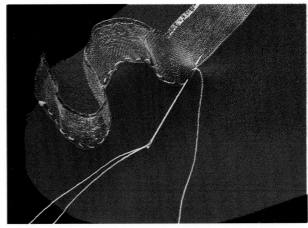

1) **Mark** shape of barrette on wrong side of fabric, using pencil or fabric marker; position barrette on bias grainline. Cut ½" (1.3 cm) outside marked line.

2) **Hand-stitch** embellishments, if desired, to barrette fabric; attach sheer ribbon by stitching one edge to right side of fabric in random design, making sure ends of ribbon are outside marked line.

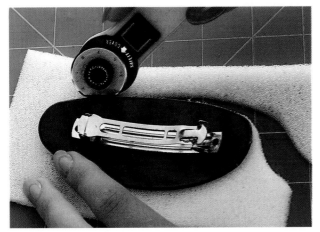

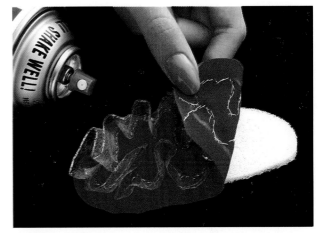

3) **Spread** a light layer of craft glue on top of barrette; position barrette on piece of polyurethane foam. Cut foam even with edges of barrette.

4) **Apply** a light layer of spray adhesive to foam; secure to wrong side of fabric, centering barrette.

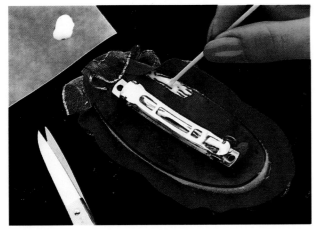

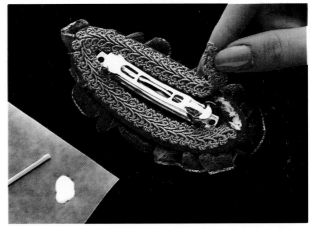

5) **Wrap** fabric to back of barrette; glue in place, applying craft glue to barrette. Trim and clip fabric as necessary for smooth wrap.

6) **Glue** gimp around back of barrette, covering the raw edges of the fabric.

Beaded Barrettes

Make beaded barrettes using vinyl cross-stitch canvas. Chart a design on graph paper, in 11 rows of 47 squares or 12 rows of 48 squares, depending on whether an odd or even number of squares is desired. Or apply the beads in a random design. The finished barrette is about 1" × 3½" (2.5 × 9 cm).

Use a short beading needle and a single strand of cotton-wrapped polyester thread. Allow at least ⅜" (1 cm) of cross-stitch canvas around the edges of the design for finishing the barrette.

YOU WILL NEED

Vinyl cross-stitch canvas, 14 count.

Seed beads; short beading needle; cotton-wrapped polyester thread.

Spring barrette clip, about 3" (7.5 cm) long.

Leather or synthetic suede scrap, for backing.

Thick craft glue, or hot glue gun and glue sticks.

How to Make a Beaded Barrette

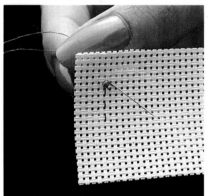

1) Weave needle through canvas to anchor thread, bringing needle up at upper left corner of design. Take diagonal stitch down through bead and to the right. Bring needle up at upper left corner of next square.

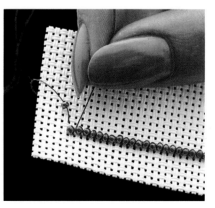

2) Continue to end of first row; bring needle down to wrong side at last bead. Turn canvas upside down for second row, so stitching will be in same direction. Repeat to complete all rows; secure thread.

3) Trim vinyl ⅜" (1 cm) from edges of design; trim corners. Fold under edges; glue in place, using craft glue or hot glue. Cut backing to size of design; glue to canvas. Glue barrette clip to backing.

88

Tulle & Ribbon Hair Bows

Feminine, romantic hair bows can be made from layers of tulle, ribbons, and decorative trims. Select trims in black and gold for a striking evening accent, or in soft pastels for an ingenue look.

The tulle, available in many colors, provides a full background for the ribbons and trims. Layer lengths of any dominant ribbons or trims, and accent them with several layers of narrow trims, such as ribbons, decorative cords, or strands of pearls or beads.

YOU WILL NEED

Tulle, two pieces about 6" × 40" (15 × 102 cm) each.
Ribbons and trims as desired, in 1⅛-yd. (1.05 m) lengths.
Spring barrette clip, about 3" (7.5 cm) long.
Beading or millinery wire.

How to Make a Tulle and Ribbon Hair Bow

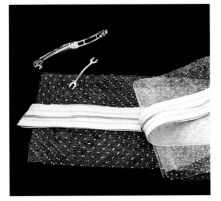

1) Cut and layer two 6" × 40" (15 × 102 cm) strips of tulle. Layer trims over tulle as desired, placing narrow trims on top. Open spring barrette clip, and remove tension bar.

2) Gather trims 4" (10 cm) from one end; secure to barrette clip with wire. Gather trims 6" (15 cm) from secured wire, forming loop; secure to barrette clip.

3) Continue to gather and secure four more loops, leaving tail at end. Replace tension bar. Fan out trims and ribbons, alternating sides.

Chiffon Hair Bows

For a classic hair bow, make either a looped-style or a circular-style bow from chiffon. Other lightweight sheer or silky fabrics, such as China silk, georgette, or charmeuse, may also be used.

Both styles of bows are easily made by wiring a single strip of fabric to a spring barrette clip; a narrow hem (page 51) finishes the edges of the fabric. If desired, a circular bow may be embellished with artificial flowers.

YOU WILL NEED

⅜ yd. (0.35 m) fabric, such as chiffon, China silk, georgette, or charmeuse.
Spring barrette clip, about 3" (7.5 cm) long.
Beading or millinery wire.
Hot glue gun and glue sticks.

How to Make a Looped-style Hair Bow

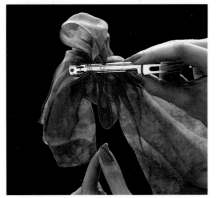  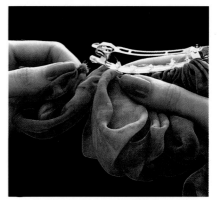

1) Hem long edges of 10" × 36" (25.5 × 91.5 cm) fabric piece (page 51). Open barrette clip; remove tension bar. Gather fabric 6" (15 cm) from one end; secure to clip with wire. Gather the fabric 6" (15 cm) away, forming loop; secure to clip.

2) Continue to gather and secure loops at 6" (15 cm) intervals, leaving 6" (15 cm) tail at end.

3) Gather one end of fabric piece; secure gathers with thread or wire. Fold under end of fabric, forming loop; secure to end of clip with hot glue. Repeat at the opposite end. Replace tension bar.

How to Make a Circular-style Hair Bow

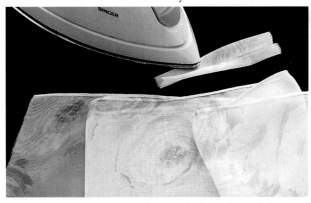 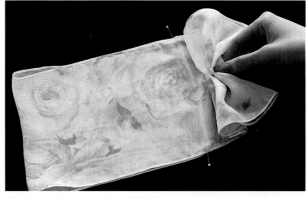

1) Hem the long edges of 7½" × 34" (19.3 × 86.5 cm) fabric piece for the bow (page 51). Press 2" × 4" (5 × 10 cm) fabric strip in half lengthwise for center wrap. Open strip; fold and press raw edges to center fold to make ½" (1.3 cm) strip.

2) Stitch short ends of fabric piece for bow, right sides together, in narrow seam. Position tube, right side out, with seam centered on bottom. Open the barrette clip, and remove tension bar. Gather fabric by hand, starting at center of one folded edge.

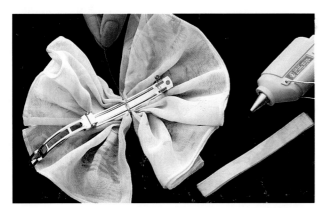 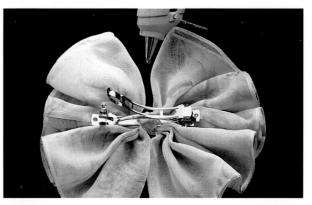

3) Secure gathered fabric to center of barrette clip, using wire. Wrap fabric strip around center of bow, securing with hot glue on back of barrette; trim excess fabric strip.

4) Glue fabric to ends of barrette clip. Glue fabric at folded edges together, just above and below center strip. Replace tension bar.

Jewelry & More

Polymer Clay Jewelry

Make your own jewelry and buttons, using polymer clay such as Fimo® or Sculpey®. Polymer clay is a modeling compound that is available in a wide range of colors at craft stores and stores specializing in miniatures. Pieces of polymer clay adhere to each other with light pressure, making it easy to design unique jewelry items. It hardens to a smooth, matte finish when oven-baked, maintaining its prebaked size.

Jewelry pieces are designed using three basic forms of clay: the ball, the rod, and the sheet. Simple balls of clay can be used for beads, or they can be flattened and shaped to form discs for buttons or earrings. Rods of clay are sliced into discs or cut and rolled to form uniform balls. Sheets of clay can be rolled and cut out, cookie-style, for buttons, pins, or earrings.

Rods and sheets can also be used to create designs. Marbleized clay is formed by twisting rods together. Patterned designs, such as a bull's-eye or pinwheel, are formed using rods and sheets. These patterned designs are called *canes*. Thin slices cut from canes are used to embellish base pieces of clay.

Different brands of polymer clay vary in firmness. To make a firm clay easier to shape, soften it by cutting it into small pieces, warming them in your hands, and kneading the pieces together. Or mix a firm clay with a softer clay until you have a consistency that is easy to work with. A firm colored clay can be mixed with a small amount of a soft white clay without sacrificing the brightness of the color.

Work on a clean, smooth surface, such as laminated plastic, marble, or ceramic. Use a lint-free cloth and petroleum jelly to clean any residue from your hands or tools when changing colors.

Bake finished pieces in a 225°F (107°C) preheated oven on a baking sheet lined with cardboard. For most pieces, 15 to 20 minutes is a sufficient baking time; thicker pieces may require more time. Pieces may be rebaked at the same temperature if they feel soft after they have cooled. A sealer or floor wax can be applied to finished pieces of polymer clay jewelry for added sheen.

YOU WILL NEED

Polymer clay.

Brayer, metal or marble rolling pin, or smooth glass jar, for rolling out sheets of polymer clay.

Single-edge wallpaper or razor blade, or sharp, thin paring knife.

Awl or nail, for puncturing holes in beads and buttons.

Baking sheet; piece of cardboard.

Sealer intended for polymer clay, or floor wax, optional for shiny surface.

Jewelry findings; jewelry glue.

Three Basic Methods for Shaping Polymer Clay

Balls. Shape polymer clay into balls by rolling small pieces of the clay between palms; keep the ball of clay moving in a circular pattern.

Rods. Roll polymer clay into even rods, using pressure of hands to control the diameter of the rod.

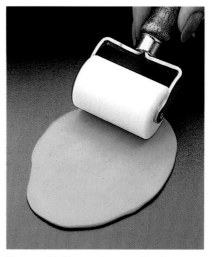

Sheets. Roll out sheets of polymer clay, using a brayer or rolling pin; turn clay over frequently, lightly pressing one edge of clay to surface before rolling.

Forms of polymer clay include (left to right) marbleized clay rod, bull's-eye cane, pinwheel cane, and striped canes. Inlays (at far right) are pressed into a clay base.

Shaping Polymer Clay for Jewelry

After learning a few simple techniques, you will be able to create a variety of jewelry pieces. The creative necklaces, bracelets, and pins shown on pages 100 to 103 are all made from shaped polymer clay.

Marbleized clay is easy to make and has design interest. It can be shaped into balls, rods, and sheets, using any of the basic methods on page 95.

More advanced designs can be achieved with the use of patterned canes, such as bull's-eye, pinwheel, and striped canes. Canes are versatile for many jewelry items; buttons and earrings can be made from sliced

pieces of a cane. A sliced cane can also be used to add inlays to jewelry.

Inlays are simply thin pieces of polymer clay that are pressed onto a polymer clay base. Inlays can be embedded flush with the surface or left slightly raised for texture.

When making patterned canes, form the cane in the largest design size desired; the remainder of the cane can later be rolled smaller. If the cane loses its shape when cut, allow the polymer clay to set overnight or refrigerate it until firm.

How to Make Marbleized Polymer Clay

1) Roll each color of polymer clay into a rod; place rods together lengthwise.

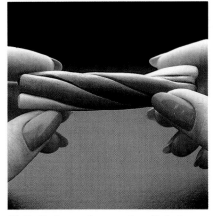

2) Roll the rods together lightly; lift, and twist ends in opposite directions. Roll lightly.

3) Roll and twist rod until desired effect is achieved; fold cane in half as necessary. Do not overwork, to prevent colors from blending. Shape into balls, rods, or sheets (page 95).

How to Make a Bull's-eye Cane

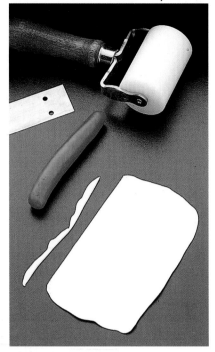

1) Shape polymer clay into a rod; this will be used for the center dot. Roll a sheet large enough to wrap around rod. Trim one long edge straight, using wallpaper blade.

2) Wrap sheet around rod, starting at long edge and pressing lightly to prevent air pockets; trim the excess clay so edges of sheet butt together. Lightly roll cane smooth.

3) Roll and wrap additional sheets around cane, if desired. Trim off distorted ends, using wallpaper blade. For canes of different sizes, roll segments into smaller diameters.

How to Make a Pinwheel Cane

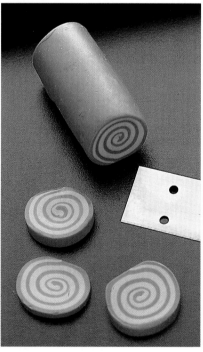

1) Roll two or three contrasting colors of polymer clay into thin rectangular sheets. Stack layers together. Trim edges of clay, using wallpaper blade.

2) Roll sheets together lengthwise; press lightly when rolling to prevent air pockets.

3) Trim off distorted ends, and slice cane, using wallpaper blade. For canes of different sizes, roll segments into smaller diameters.

How to Make a Striped Cane

 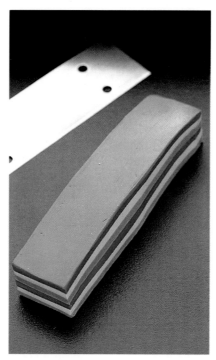 

1) Roll desired colors of polymer clay into thin rectangular sheets. Stack layers together; press lightly. Trim edges, using wallpaper blade.

2) Cut layers lengthwise, and restack; press together lightly. Repeat as desired; layers can be stacked in different arrangements.

3) Wrap cane, if desired, as in steps 1 and 2 for bulls-eye cane, opposite. Compress the cane by uniformly pressing sides, using a book wrapped in plastic. Slice cane.

How to Inlay Designs

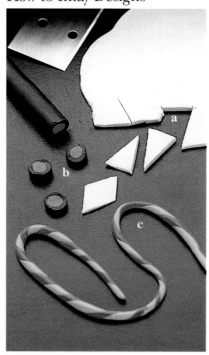  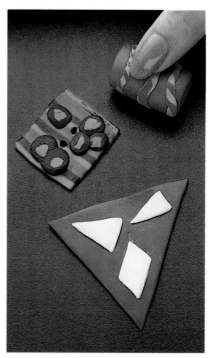

1) Make inlay shapes from thin sheets of polymer clay **(a)**, thin slices of bull's-eye, pinwheel, or striped canes **(b)**, or small rods of marbleized clay **(c)**.

2) Position inlays as desired onto clay base; press lightly to secure.

3) Embed inlays in rounded piece by gently rolling it. Embed inlays in flat pieces by lightly pressing, without distorting base. Inlays may remain slightly raised.

Making Jewelry & Buttons

Polymer clay is easily made into necklaces, bracelets, earrings, pins, and buttons. Start with small, simple projects, and add inlays as embellishments. Experiment with shaping and twisting the pieces of clay to vary the shapes of the jewelry pieces. Attach findings to baked jewelry pieces, using craft glue.

Polymer clay buttons should be hand washed. Do not place the buttons in a hot dryer.

Tips for Making Necklaces and Bracelets

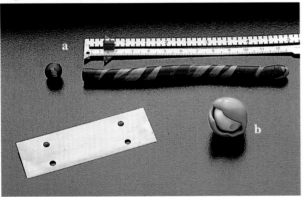

Make uniform beads by marking marbleized or solid-colored clay rod into even increments; slice at marks **(a)**. Or for large, lightweight beads, cover wooden beads with bits of clay; roll smooth with hands **(b)**.

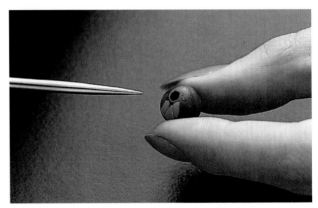

Puncture beads on one side, using awl large enough to accommodate cording; remove awl, and insert again from opposite side. Bake (page 95).

String baked beads for bracelets and short necklaces on round cord elastic, and knot. Secure knot with craft glue. Conceal knot by sliding it into bead.

String baked beads for long necklaces on strong decorative cording, such as rattail or leather. Secure knot with craft glue.

Make bangle bracelets, covering cardboard or wooden bracelets with flattened bits of clay. Press clay in place evenly. Bake (page 95).

Tips for Making Earrings and Pins

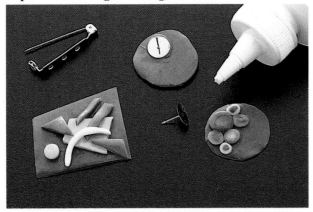

Shape earrings and pins from balls of polymer clay flattened into discs. Add inlays for more texture and design. Bake (page 95). Center and secure earring backs or pin back near the top, using craft glue.

Make collage-style pins, cutting pieces from polymer clay sheets. Smooth the cut edges with fingers. Bake (page 95). Center and secure pin back near top of pin, using craft glue.

Tips for Making Buttons

Shape buttons from flattened marbleized clay or from slices of a cane or sheet. Pierce holes in the buttons, using an awl. Bake (page 95).

Make button cover by forming polymer clay over metal base; trim excess even with edge. Open cover, indenting clay at hinge. Bake (page 95).

Tips for Embellishing Jewelry

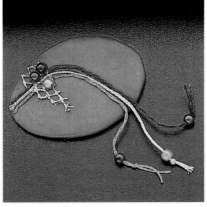

Create imprints in unbaked clay, using cut glass, textured fabric, screening, or another raised surface.

Embellish unbaked clay pieces with beads and bits of fibers, embedding them into the clay. Any item that can withstand 225°F (107°C) can be baked into the piece.

Add sheen to the baked pieces, if desired, using floor wax applied with fingers or using a sealer intended for use with polymer clay.

Necklaces can be made in a variety of styles. A large wooden bead, covered with a layer of polymer clay and embellished with inlays of stripes and pinwheels, creates a simple pendant (top). Another necklace is created from beads in a variety of sizes and shapes; a large, flattened bead and several smaller beads are secured to the ends of the cording, creating a focal point (middle). Inlaid beads made from polymer clay are combined with purchased beads to quickly create a long necklace (bottom).

Ideas for Polymer Clay Jewelry

The pieces of jewelry shown here combine various techniques for shaping polymer clay. Even those that look intricate in design are actually easy to make. Be creative in the use of color and design.

Bracelet is inlaid with slices from a variety of pinwheel and striped canes. Slices from the striped cane were manipulated for a curved, flowing pattern.

Earrings were created from sheets of solid-colored clay and slices of pinwheels; texture was added to the solid-colored clay, using lace. Metallic cord, threaded through holes, secures the pieces.

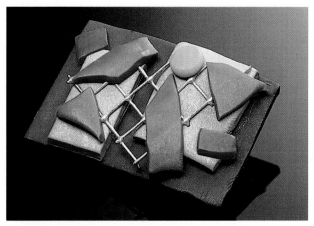

Collage-style pin is designed from simple shapes cut from sheets of polymer clay. Combined with wire mesh, the small pieces were embedded in the clay base.

Earrings with dangles are made from cutouts of clay sheets and polymer clay beads. The dangles are attached to the earring base.

Button Jewelry

Button jewelry is fast and easy to make. Jewelry findings can be attached to buttons to make earrings, pins, tie tacks, and stick pins. Use button pins to adorn garments, embellish purses and belts, and hold scarves in place. Button jewelry can be made inexpensively using extra buttons from sewing projects. Or showcase unusual or antique buttons by turning them into one-of-a-kind jewelry pieces.

Old buttons offer unusual details and craftsmanship; combining one or two with new buttons can make jewelry pieces unique. Look for old buttons at flea markets, antique stores, and thrift shops.

When designing button jewelry, include buttons that vary in color, size, shape, or texture, using special buttons as a focal point. Keep earrings and pins light in weight if you intend to use them on lightweight fabrics. Design the button jewelry so the finished piece has a flat base to which you can secure the jewelry findings.

Button jewelry can be assembled using hot glue or jewelry glue. Buttons can be glued together, using larger buttons to form the foundation. Or glue the buttons to a decorative base, such as a shell or a decorative belt buckle.

YOU WILL NEED

Variety of buttons.

Jewelry findings, such as pin back, earring backs, or stick pin.

Hot glue gun and glue sticks, or jewelry glue.

Ideas for Using Button Jewelry

Lapel pin and earrings, made from coordinating buttons, dress up a basic suit.

Scarf pin, consisting of a buckle and small, decorative buttons, secures a scarf at the neckline.

How to Make Button Jewelry

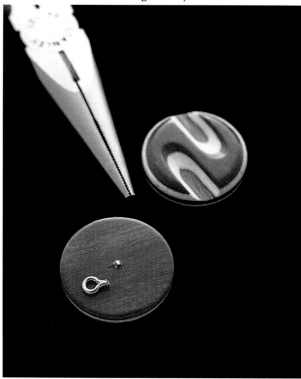

1) **Remove** shanks from buttons, if necessary, using a wire cutter. File the back of the button smooth.

2) **Glue** buttons, working from the bottom layer to the top, allowing the glue to dry thoroughly between layers. Glue jewelry finding to back.

Tips for Designing Button Jewelry

Use sewing notions, such as snaps or hooks and eyes, to add an interesting accent and to fill small spaces.

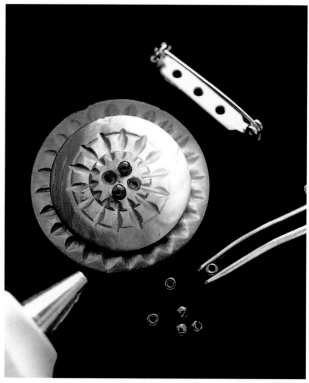

Conceal holes in buttons with beads or rhinestones; secure, using glue and tweezers.

Combine parts of old jewelry with buttons to create one-of-a-kind pieces.

Stack and glue buttons in graduated sizes to a large button base.

Add dangles from old jewelry. Or create your own dangles, using decorative threads or leather strips; add beads, if desired. Glue dangles to back of jewelry.

Glue decorative trim, such as ruched ribbon, to the back of large button. Cut a backing circle from leather, and glue to button back; secure jewelry finding.

Fiber Jewelry

Jewelry made from fibers and fabric scraps provides the perfect match to garments that you sew. Or use the wide choice of colors available in fabrics and decorative threads to make coordinating jewelry for purchased garments.

Make several styles of pins, earrings, and bracelets to add variety when accessorizing your wardrobe. The projects on the following pages require minimal materials and are fast and easy to make.

1) Origami-style jewelry uses paper-folding techniques to create pins and earrings.

2) Fabric collage earrings and pins allow you to combine a variety of fabrics for a customized match to garments. Dimensional fabric paint seals the raw edges of the fabrics.

3) Jewelry from leather, with fibers and feathers added, has a dimensional, textured effect.

4) Wire mesh earrings are created from hardware cloth, leather or fabric strips, decorative threads, and beads.

5) Fabric-wrapped bracelets offer textural interest. The fabric strips are torn and wrapped around inexpensive bangle bracelets.

Origami-style Jewelry

This folded-fabric jewelry is fashioned after Japanese *origami*, or paper folding. Contrasting fabrics are fused together and then folded. One fused square forms an earring, or two squares are positioned together to form a pin.

This technique is suitable for lightweight, tightly woven fabrics. To emphasize the Oriental look, use scraps of silk; hand-dyed silk (page 63) adds visual interest to the jewelry. Or choose a printed fabric, and combine it with a coordinating solid color.

YOU WILL NEED

Two contrasting lightweight fabric scraps.

Lightweight fusible web.

Decorative thread.

Decorative button, for pin.

Jewelry findings, such as pin back or earring backs.

Thick craft glue.

Liquid fray preventer.

Origami-style jewelry is made from folded fabric and resembles Japanese origami. The pin (above) is made from fine cotton. The earrings (left) are made from hand-dyed silk.

How to Make Origami-style Pin or Earrings

1) Cut two sets of two contrasting squares, cutting them on straight of grain; cut 4" (10 cm) squares for earrings, or 4½" (11.5 cm) for pin. Cut two squares from fusible web slightly smaller than fabric.

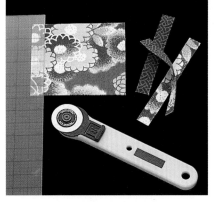

2) Fuse two contrasting squares of fabric, wrong sides together, using fusible web. Repeat for remaining squares of fabric. Trim ½" (1.3 cm) from all edges of each fused square.

3) Fold square in half diagonally without creasing fold; the finished look of the jewelry depends on which fabric is folded to the inside.

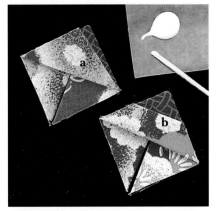

4) Fold triangle in half. Placing finger under upper layer, hold lower three layers in position.

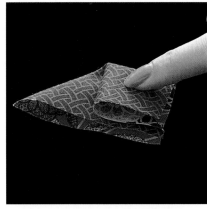

5) Flatten upper portion into a square; hold in position. Lightly press folded edges of square.

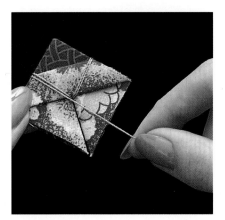

6) Flatten the opposite side into a square, turning the piece over. Lightly press.

7) Fold upper layer of fabric in half diagonally **(a).** Form flap by folding point under to foldline **(b).** Repeat for flap on opposite side. Glue the folded flaps down.

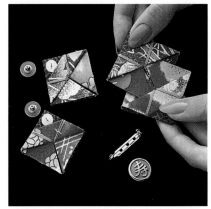

8) Trim any loose threads; apply liquid fray preventer to raw edges. Wrap decorative thread as shown, to secure folded layers; alternate sides when wrapping. Tie ends of thread on back side.

9) Glue earring backs at the upper corners. For pin, slide two folded squares together, inserting loose triangles into pockets; glue in place. Glue button at center of pin; glue pin back near upper edge.

Fabric Collage Jewelry

Fabric scraps, glued together for a collage effect, can be used to create a variety of pin and earring styles. The edges of the fabric are decoratively sealed with dimensional paint.

Cut the fabric into different sizes and shapes, such as rectangles and triangles, and experiment with various arrangements to find the combination you like best. If you are using lightweight fabric, such as silk or lamé, fuse a lightweight interfacing to the wrong side of the fabric before cutting the shapes.

YOU WILL NEED

Fabric scraps.

Firm, nonwoven, sew-in interfacing.

Lightweight fusible interfacing, if lightweight, silky fabric is used.

Leather or synthetic suede scrap, for backing.

Dimensional fabric paint.

Jewelry findings, such as pin back or earring backs.

Thick craft glue.

How to Make Fabric Collage Jewelry

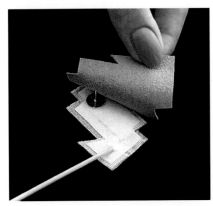

1) Cut fabric shapes in various sizes, as desired; for earrings, cut two of each shape, with fabric right sides together. Arrange the shapes into desired collage, overlapping edges; earrings can be mirror images.

2) Glue the overlapping edges of the collage pieces together; allow to dry.

3) Mark outer edge of collage on sew-in interfacing, using a pencil. Cut interfacing ⅛" (3 mm) inside marked line. Glue interfacing to back of collage.

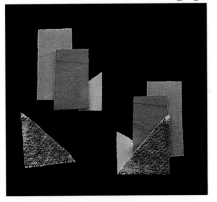

4) Glue jewelry finding near upper edge on back of collage; allow to dry. Cut the leather slightly larger than collage; cut a hole in leather for jewelry finding. Glue leather to collage, wrong sides together.

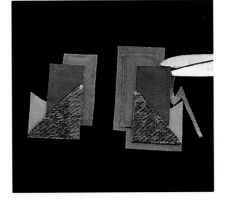

5) Trim edges of leather even with outer edges of collage; angle blades slightly so leather does not show from right side of jewelry. Round corners and points, if desired.

6) Outline all fabric edges with dimensional fabric paint. Allow paint to dry.

Jewelry from Leather

Small scraps of leather, layered and combined with decorative ribbons, threads, feathers, or other items, become distinctive pins and earrings. For additional texture and color, unwaxed leather can be embellished with fabric paints.

Leather scraps are available at leather craft stores and through mail-order suppliers. Choose scraps in a variety of colors or textures. For large jewelry pieces, use a firm piece of leather for the lining to give support to the jewelry.

When designing leather jewelry, cut the leather pieces into a variety of shapes. You may want to experiment with construction paper before cutting the leather. Add interest to a pair of earrings by making one earring slightly different from the other.

YOU WILL NEED

Leather scraps.
Embellishments, such as ribbons, feathers, and decorative threads.
Thick craft glue.
Jewelry findings, such as pin back or earring backs.

How to Make Jewelry from Leather

1) Determine the base shape of the jewelry piece, and cut a scrap of leather to this size. Earrings can be mirror images.

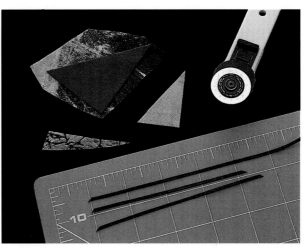

2) Cut and arrange additional leather pieces on the base piece, working from largest to smallest piece; layer embellishments as desired between leather pieces.

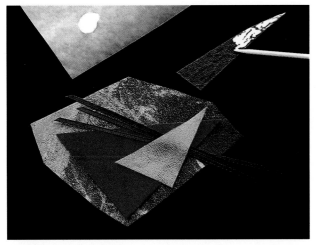

3) Glue pieces together, using a thin layer of glue on the back of each piece.

4) Glue pin back or earring back to base piece, near upper edge; allow to dry.

5) Cut a leather lining slightly larger than base; cut a hole in lining for the pin back or earring back. Glue lining to base, wrong sides together.

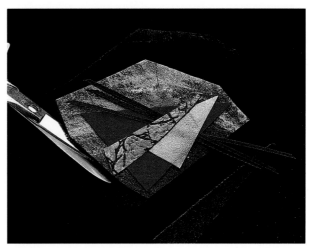

6) Trim edges of lining even with base, using sharp scissors; angle blades slightly so lining does not show from right side of jewelry.

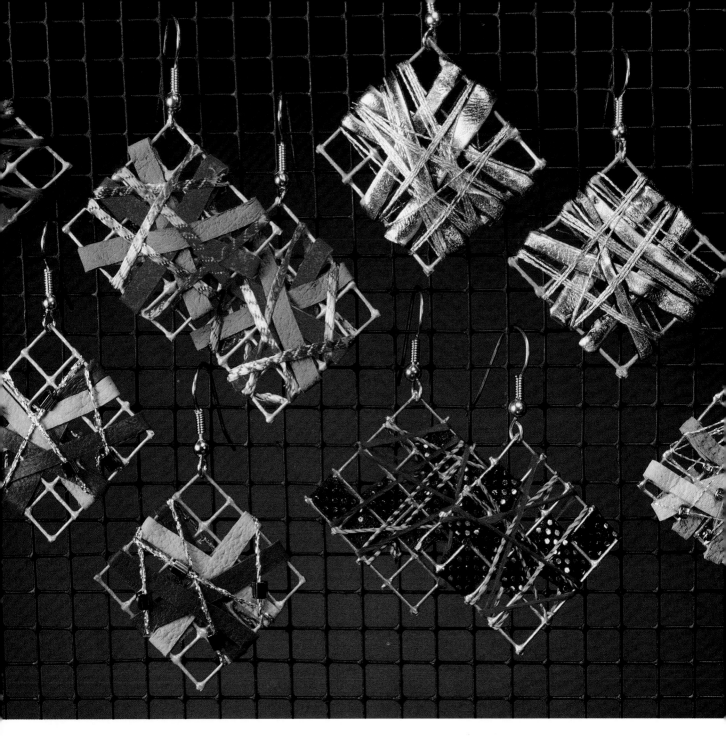

Wire Mesh Earrings

Create contemporary-style earrings from a wire mesh called *hardware cloth*, available from hardware stores, and strips of fabric or leather. These earrings are simple and inexpensive, and can be made to match or coordinate with a favorite outfit.

Hardware cloth is available only in silver, but may be painted gold. It provides a base for weaving or wrapping narrow strips of lightweight fabric or leather. Decorative threads, wrapped over the fabric or leather, provide additional interest, and beads can be used as accents.

YOU WILL NEED

Hardware cloth with ¼" (6 mm) grid.
Fabric or leather scraps.
Decorative threads.
Metal file; wire cutter; needlenose pliers.
Gold metallic acrylic paint and small paintbrush, optional.
Earring findings.
Thick craft glue.

How to Make Wire Mesh Earrings

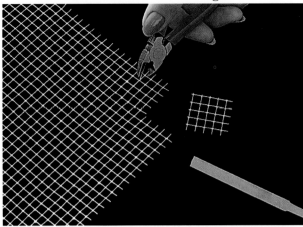

Earrings with fabric. 1) Cut two 1" (2.5 cm) squares from hardware cloth, using wire cutter. Smooth edges, using metal file.

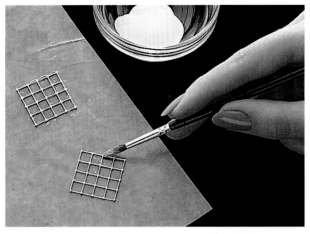

2) Paint the hardware cloth, if desired, using gold metallic paint; allow paint to dry.

3) Cut one ¼" × 6" (6 mm × 15 cm) strip of fabric for each earring; weave through grid, using a large-eyed needle or small crochet hook. Trim any excess fabric at ends; secure ends with glue.

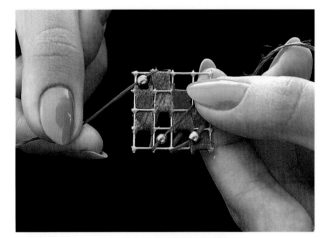

4) Wrap decorative thread randomly around hardware cloth, adding beads, if desired. Glue or knot ends of thread on back side of earring.

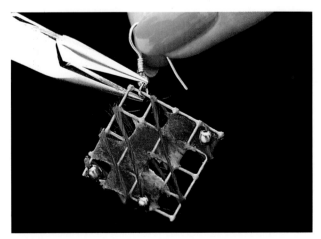

5) Attach earring finding to corner of hardware cloth, using needlenose pliers.

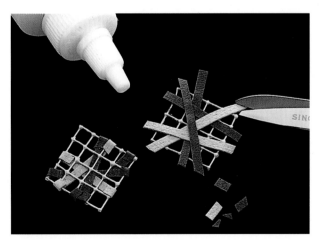

Earrings with leather. Follow steps 1 and 2. Cut four to six ⅛" × 1¾" (3 mm × 4.5 cm) leather strips; wrap strips around hardware cloth as desired. Trim ends, fold under, and glue. Complete as in steps 4 and 5.

Fabric-wrapped Bracelets

Use leftover fabrics to make bracelets that coordinate with your garments. These fabric-wrapped bracelets are quickly made, using inexpensive bangle bracelets and two narrow strips of fabric. The strips are torn, adding texture to the bracelet. You may want to make a set of bracelets, reversing the order in which the strips are wrapped or combining different fabrics.

Choose soft, lightweight fabrics that can be torn into narrow strips. Sueded silks and rayons work well and add subtle color shading. When wrapping a bracelet, stretch the fabric strips taut to prevent the fabric from shifting when the bracelet is completed.

YOU WILL NEED

Fabric scraps.

Plastic or wooden bangle bracelet with rounded surface, at least ¾" (2 cm) wide.

Decorative rayon cording.

Fabric glue or thick craft glue.

How to Make a Fabric-wrapped Bracelet

1) Tear one 1" × 36" (2.5 × 91.5 cm) strip of fabric for first layer; tear one ½" × 36" (1.3 × 91.5 cm) strip of contrasting fabric for second layer. Glue wrong side of one end of 1" (2.5 cm) strip to inside of bracelet, positioning fabric at an angle.

2) Wrap fabric around bracelet, angling fabric and overlapping edges; trim excess fabric, and glue end to inside of bracelet.

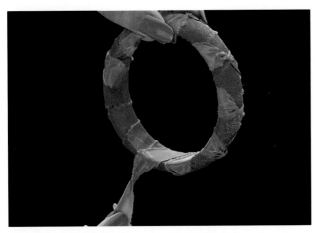

3) Glue wrong side of one end of ½" (1.3 cm) strip to inside of bracelet, with fabric angled in opposite direction from first fabric. Wrap strip at an angle, twisting fabric once or twice on outside of bracelet. Trim excess fabric; glue end to inside.

4) Wrap rayon cording around bracelet as desired. Glue ends of cording to inside of bracelet.

Sunglasses

Create your own designer frames by embellishing inexpensive sunglasses. Sunglasses can become a fun, flashy accessory or a finishing touch for a special ensemble. Use items such as buttons, beads, rhinestones, decorative threads, and strips of leather. A few items are usually all that is necessary.

When applying embellishments with glue, make sure the base of the item rests flat on the surface of the frame, to ensure good adhesion. Use a jewelry glue intended for plastics and metals, working carefully to avoid excess glue on the frames. You may want to work with a tweezers and apply the glue using a toothpick.

Buttons add a simple embellishment to sunglasses. Remove the shanks from the buttons, using a wire cutter, and apply the buttons with glue.

Beads, gems, and painted designs are easy-to-add accents for sunglasses.

Gloves

Gloves can be fashionable accessories, not simply functional apparel. Whether you choose vivid, colorful gloves or opt for the ever-popular basic colors, a few embellishments can add style.

Decorative braid trims can be machine-stitched in place along the upper edge of the gloves. When attaching trims to knit gloves, make sure that the embellished gloves retain enough stretch to be

pulled on and off easily. For leather gloves, machine-stitch the trim in place, using a leather needle, or secure it with a glue intended for leather.

Buttons add a whimsical look to a glove. Choose buttons that will lie flat. Stitch them in place, one at a time, without carrying threads between them, to prevent catching the threads when putting on the gloves. This also ensures the necessary give between buttons.

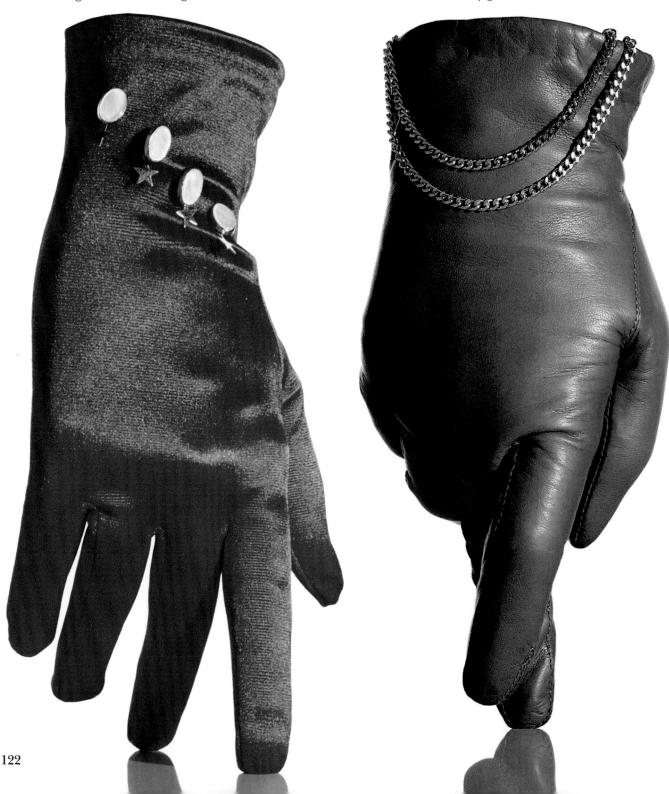

Shown left to right:

Small, charm-style buttons are stitched to stretch-knit gloves in a diagonal row.

Gold chains drape softly at the wrist like bracelets. The chains are simply hand-tacked in place to the inside of the glove at the upper edge.

Three large buttons are an elegant embellishment for a simple pair of stretch-knit gloves. Select buttons that will lie flat against the gloves.

Braid and gimp trims, machine-stitched in place at the upper edge, complement a pair of classic leather gloves. The small tassel, hand-stitched at the side of the glove, adds a final touch.

Beaded appliqués or decorative buttons can become shoe clips by simply stitching covered coat hooks to the underside of the appliqués or buttons.

Shoes

Use your creativity to embellish shoes so they coordinate with special outfits. Elegant appliqués can adorn the toe areas, or rhinestones can add unexpected glitz at the heels. Many decorations are easy to add, but you may prefer to have some embellishments stitched or stapled in place by a shoe repair service.

For special occasions, use shoe clips as temporary shoe decorations. They can be made using the hook portion of large covered hooks and eyes, called coat hooks. When attaching the shoe clips to the shoes, squeeze the hooks as necessary to hold the clips in place. To temporarily secure lightweight items, such as sequined appliqués, use double-stick tape.

When using glue to attach embellishments, select a glue that will dry clear and flexible, such as Tacky® glue. Avoid gluing embellishments to an area where they are apt to be rubbed off, or to areas where the shoes will flex when worn.

Paints can add a decorative flourish of color to shoes. When painting shoes, it is important that the paint remain flexible on the shoe. For this reason, textile paints are recommended for fabric shoes; heat-set the paint with a hair dryer. Acrylic paints are recommended for leather shoes. You may want to test a small amount of the paint in an inconspicuous area, because paint may not adhere to some highly waxed leathers.

Sequined appliqués can be held in place with double-stick tape to provide a temporary shoe decoration for a special occasion.

Textile paints are applied to canvas shoes in a color-blocked design. Using tape, mask off any areas of the shoe that will not be painted.

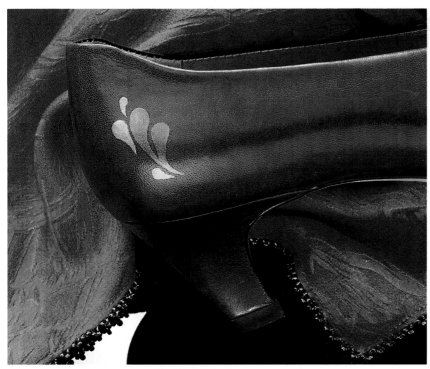

Painted accents add a splash of color at the outside heel area. For leather shoes, acrylic paints are recommended.

Rhinestones, glued in place, dress up a pair of basic pumps, as shown at right.

Index

For more information about the
fashion accessories available from
these designers, call 1-800-328-3895.

Beaded Barrettes
   Gayle Liman
Button Jewelry
   Kathy Tilton
Fabric Collage Jewelry
   Kathy Tilton
Hand-dyed Silk Scarves
   Melanie Teig-Schwolert
Leather Jewelry
   Kathy Tilton
Origami-style Jewelry
   Marcia Kelly
Polymer Clay Jewelry
   Barbara Hjort
Suede Belt
   Linda Nakashimi
Wire Mesh Earrings
   Marcia Kelly

Cy DeCosse Incorporated offers
a variety of how-to books. For
information write:
   Cy DeCosse Subscriber Books
   5900 Green Oak Drive
   Minnetonka, MN 55343